There was this movie poster I saw outside the cinema hall when I was about eleven years old and it pulled me like a magnet, movies were the only entertainment we had outside the house if you could afford it; it was an Indian movie so reading it made no sense, we always went to admire the actors even if we couldn't pay the entry tickets.

In the picture something stood out was the couple, a very beautiful girl with long black hair that over flowed over her shoulder, she wore a white half sleeved blazer, black long pants and a red silk top holding the arm of a handsome built man with her both hands as if using them for support leaning towards him and her head rested on his shoulder. The man's shirt was open at the chest showing muscled slightly hairy chest, he had dark eye glasses on.

The lady looked at the camera with a shy smile and her big round clear beautiful eyes were made to torment men. This was love well portrayed in the picture, without words one got enough to expect a love story in the movie with a happy ending, happily ever after kind of thing. I started longing that kind of love, I longed for a beautiful girl helplessly clinging to me and I give her the world. Well if only it was that simple in the real life.

Every morning had become a mechanical routine to me, waking up at around seven in the morning, take breakfast that was the same unless an occasion changed it: a cup of tea with a buttered toast of bread followed by a cup of fishy porridge; fishy because tiny fish were ground whole with sorghum, millet and ground nuts to make the flour- that was too much protein but it kept us strong, the fish smell in the porridge was strong and then I ate fruits. In many cases I took breakfast doing something else like sorting out fruits or cutting up fruits for salad,

I would take bites of fruits sporadically until the job was done; this would be followed by a shower and then tying them up onto the bicycle and by nine o'clock I would leave the house. I loved this breakfast, it was just after boarding high school where the breakfast was a small slice of bread and very bad tea, the food too had not changed for thirty years but the fees had changed many times, it's the story of the government schools, being in one is a privilege, take it or leave it, its not a holiday camp, it's a reminder of what your parents can afford or want for you at that particular stage; typically what they can afford. This doesn't stop some playing rich or looking rich.

We lived in a considerably big compound just next to the tarmac road though the gate was on the side of a dirt road that led to other houses mostly rentals ahead, due to demand the owners had made single rooms in their compounds to rent out instead of farming or living alone in the once what was wheat and corn farm land. College students who became mothers while still in school lived in them. One would clearly hear all cars out on the road, motorbikes and the noisy pedestrians though few, noisy people made our German shepherd dog that was growing too fast bark heavily.

The fruits I prepared in the morning were for selling, there was preparing the mixed fruit salad and sorting the whole fruits, I also made the passion fruits juice, the customers were the university students and middle working staff, the junior staff couldn't afford such a luxury and the senior staff couldn't be caught dead buying from a student centre stall.

I rode my bike loaded with fruits that were in a plastic crate through a big manned beautiful university gate - down the slope across the bridge over a small cascading soil polluted river and then up the gentle ascent, the small river at that point was almost hidden by herbaceous plants that grew over it; that river flowed to the lake thirty kilometres down stream. Upstream people used its water for consumption. The university labs had done an analysis of the water and found it not fit for humans but the users had nowhere else to get the water, actually they had warned that if the results are negative the university can flash it down their sewers but the word came out. There were no fish or frogs in the river which went far to confirm its status health wise.

The bicycle momentum down slope took me almost to the top of the ascent on the other side. With the fruits weight however I always alighted to push the crappy old bicycle by hands all the way to the fruits parlour. The uniformed guards at the main gate were used to me; sometimes I gave them fruits to be in favour with them; more like avoid getting harassed over nothing, they were quacks who believed harassing equals security, I wondered if they were hired out of idiocy rather than wit. I still meet such guards and care takers.

The university gate meant many things to many people, for the students it was a path to a bright future, for others it's a reminder of the dreams they had but never attained, for some it was a source of money in matters of business, for the teaching staff it represented power behind their academic achievements. For some it where they changed their fortunes in illegal means. There were days when the university would be ripped right, left and centre by unscrupulous people in the wrong positions that handled money. Still for some, it was the only home they knew of; the children of the housed workers; some employees never left the staff houses until retirement. For a good number including myself, it is where we found love.

This stretch of the road had tall trees at the sides and a walking pavement at the left hand side, the canopies of these trees almost touched above totally shielding the tarmac, this was a very beautiful sight. A few times it branched to the left towards the big and beautiful staff houses, the branched roads were also alternative routes depending on where you were going within the expanse of the university. The grass was well manicured at every inch and the flowers that were evenly spaced well trimmed. It was serenity at its top, every damn inch of the way, on the right side at some point there were green houses then on the same side ahead was the main playing field that was expansive and therapeutic as seen through the tall spaced trees. At the end of the field were basket ball courts and Tennis courts. The pavilion where the audience sat as they watched the sports was closer to the road which also was a beautiful building. The compound was ever green not that watering was ever done but the climate was cool and the area received adequate rainfall. Those who visited for the first time were overtaken by the beauty and the greenery that was utterly breathtaking. I was used to it after some time, I hardly looked at it with awe as I did the first days but humans do get used to beautiful things to a point of taking them for granted, don't they?. To the left of the tennis courts was the swimming pool adjacent to a beautiful building that was out of bounds to the students, it was a research centre with hostels that housed foreigners or high profile visitors. After the swimming pool on the same side was the transport department with many buses and other university cars parked inside for service or just parking.

Not a week had passed when my fruits fell off and sprawled all over as I alighted up the slope. The worst that fell was the fruits salad from a clear plastic storage container; I used to carry it prepared from home.

Half of it could not be salvaged. Young babies used to be introduced fruits in such a mix, fruit salad was still a new thing to adults and that's why curious eyes looked at me wondering why I had it with me in such amounts. It was so humiliating and although it was a cold morning. This part of pushing the bicycle to me was the worst part of the job; it was a bit embarrassing meeting university students going to classes as I pushed the fruits loaded bicycle. Later I had a guy doing the pushing job for me.

I started sweating and wondering why would such happen to me; a psychology lecturer that knew me found me picking fruits and stopped his car, he offered to carry the fruits in the trunk of his beige coloured 405 Peugeot car, he was such a humble good man; it was beyond what many people of his social class would do. He came from money; his father a former politician had a big wheat farm not far off that had been bought from a white settler that's why his help and humility was of even a bigger significance. Some folks who felt like demigods by working in the university would not even look at me at such a situation, even if they grew up poor. All the same, the day would end on a very happy note. They say that you don't curse a day until it's over. Anything can happen to change your fate.

Love is colourful, love is blind, love is sweet, love is complicated, love can hurt like nothing else, love can heal, love can kill and sometimes it has a colour which is white and black just to say the least; its the most complex subject that exists, poets, authors, singers, great orators and motivational speakers all have had an input on the infinite subject. Love never knocks; it hits hard and breaks doors without apologies. Some people have created master pieces, crossed seas, committed suicide, started wars like in the case of Helen of Troy; all in the name of love. If you have never been a victim, you don't know what I am talking about but if you know, you know. It is what it is when it comes blasting through the door of your fragile heart and this would be my case.

I grew up in the neighborhood of the Egerton University, some universities form a cosmopolitan community in the surrounding areas that is unique in a way, its heavily dependant on the well being of the university, the university attracted an urban set up from what was previously an agricultural land around it full of hostel rooms, rental houses, businesses and then residential homes to the employees. We walked in and out of the institution all the time without restrictions unlike nowadays, we became part of this after my brother became a student while I was still young and he got employed in the same university. I was just a small curious boy by the time he graduated. We loved the environment and by the time I was in high school I could study in a lecture room; Holland hall that was a theater room, I loved to go up the steps and study in this sound proofed room and just get amazed by its beauty and craftsmanship employed while building it, it had that old mastery touch that hasn't been replaced by the modern technology. I was determined that this is the campus I would like to study at; it was the only one I had visited but I was totally in love with it.

Egerton- the institution of higher learning has a love story behind it incase you all didn't know, its named after a man that came with colonizers from England and the bastard gave himself thousands of hectares of agricultural land just like his white friends displacing the locals with the power of the gun, actually the whole of that area more that a hundred kilometres radius leaks of former colonizers settlements and on some sides it stretches to hundreds of kilometres, there are remnants of their houses. Egerton built a forty room mansion master piece in a castle style for his bride to be who was back in England, there were servants in their quarters metres away, horses to carry the bride around the ranch and every good thing that was royalty in England, he wanted to wow her with opulence and elegance. She eventually visited and never liked the jungle that his man was excited about, the man saw wealth and freedom, aristocratic life that he could only envy back home; she saw primitive life without theatre shows and carriage rides along the urban streets. He saw secluded life without any relative or neighbor snooping or judging him; she saw distance from family and friends, mostly she saw black people all around who were the servants, they irritated her for no reason.

She couldn't stay even after the grand tour of the forty room mansion that included a music room; he was so mad that later on he never wanted to deal with any woman, he died single. He had no worker who was a woman and he told those who were married and living in his quarters to keep their women out of the way whenever he walked around. He had done his best for love but it was not enough to keep his fiancée. Later he established an agricultural institution that he later left to the today is a big university with the largest land in the country, it was handed to the government which was a silver lining. After grabbing the land; he gave it back well developed. He had grown old and the only joy left to him was making someone happy and gain from his experience, money had not bought him happiness, if anything it had taken it away, he let it do that by refusing to fall in love after the heart break, the mansion where children could have played and made it alive was a very lonely place over the years. The mansion today holds parties and weddings and it is an attractive monument.

Another white settler who must have been his closest neighbor lived comfortably with his wife who fell in love with this male strong boy red bloodied male that was employed in their home. The wife made sure she was near his working area; he was strong and ate with full appetite unlike his husband who barely ate. When the lady made advances to him he did not run away leaving his cloak like Joseph of the Bible, he happily obliged and enjoyed himself like a sailor on leave until one day a gun clocked behind his head while still in the action. He stood up frozen knowing too well that the judgment day had come. The man was very just, he gave him two options, to die or get castrated, he chose the latter and the white man did the job whistling as the wife watched seemingly in amusement. 'Don't hurt him' she said 'it was my idea; he has been merciless in a good way.' The young man continued to work but he terribly feared women to his death. There was a good twist though in the story, after the country's freedom the whites gradually left the country those that never wanted to become citizens, this couple chose to leave and with one heir to their fortune, the eunuch young man; he got everything, he lived rich keeping off women until his last breath.

The university students back in the day walked around like gods; with this pride of having a great future, they were the untouchable, the Ecclesia, they were revered in the neighborhoods. I liked their sense of style especially from those that came from the city actually the rest lot were invisible socially. The way they spoke in flawless English. This was the group of young men and women handsome and beautiful without denial. They knew it and they never held back, they enhanced and nurtured their sex appeal to the dot. Some other students never liked the popular influential city groups, they found them proud and irresponsible; they called them the ozone; this referred to the layer above in the atmosphere- the untouchables but this was just a concentration of many cultural backgrounds brought together by education.

You see the city group came from the middle class of professionals and business men/women; their parents sometimes were college educated or with experience in the lucrative careers, they had gone up the social circles and their positions at work and their children had had a smooth and a privileged life.

The other group that would emerge from the country side mostly came from very humble backgrounds; not all but a big majority, they schooled by sale of farm produce and goats, many believed that everyone who made it to university was like them so this was a culture shock to them, they realized that so many of who called the shots in the campus were not country folks. They were kids who carried influence in their blood. The jobs they got again would be in the cities and they would bring a generation of privileged urban middle class kids later to the universities, it is the cycle of life.

On weekends they went out for drinks and partying, they had money to spend in many cases, student loan was well celebrated but painful to pay; why give loans to someone without a job and if he fails to pay it affects his future loans, I mean you start a job with a loan to pay, why not charge affordably?. Some would not attend college without the loan so it was useful to some while to some it was pocket money for partying. I would attend every event that was in the university while I was on high school holiday; I attended games, shows from visiting artists, plays by students....... I shared the stories and events with my friends in high school and they would study with a renewed mission; to have such a life later in campus not to have a career but to enjoy the social life there in and all my close friends all went to universities, it is called power of a vision, none of them though came to this campus which was the same I told them about.

Sometimes brawls and fights over unpaid bills or some other nonsense was common but the students remained 'mighty' in the land. Some were addicts and opportunists that had little going on for them. Some never graduated or they came back to finish up to five years later. Some sired kids even with mad women outside the campus while totally intoxicated, some ladies got married when they were students by some working men and most left without goodbye after graduation having had a free stay and food, some men were free loaders and lived with older women who owned businesses outside campus and of course they just wanted to live off the women. Some alumni settled in the neighborhoods where they operated businesses or just in employment.

Strikes and rioting as well would sometimes wreck havoc in the campus and in the neighborhood causing the campus to be closed indefinitely. Rioting students were synonymous with breaking glass windows or burning some buildings, the police would come in and whip up some as the circular was declared all to vacate indefinitely.

Police liked the whipping part and woe unto you if it landed on you. I saw Dickson who was already running away carrying two bags meet the police around a building, it was a short chase before the whip landed on his skinny butt, he dropped the bags, ran faster as he screamed and never returned to pick the bags. Such bags were sometimes stolen and other times collected and stored in custodian offices.

We hated this period; there was lifelessness and gloom in the neighborhood. For us boys we had no one to emulate, the male students set the language, the clothing style, the recent music and the lingo that mattered. Beautiful young ladies smelling nice and looking stylish were like a therapy to us, they also set the trends for teenage girls within the campus and its environs. We would keep the hope up until they come back, the last week towards campus opening the mood would change; there would be excitement in the air. It meant business back for the business oriented neighborhoods where the students shopped on daily basis. It meant style, it meant vibrancy and we loved it.

In my final year in high school, my brother went back as a student for more studies, he was married by the time, married to a former student from the same campus and they lived in the city thirty kilometres away. This wasn't good if I closed school and I was far from the university. Due to the commuting distance they went closer to rent a house in the neighborhood. He even started a business inside the campus. He had stopped working to study so he needed the money from the business. They needed a reliable employee and I got my first job a month after high school. I loved the place, it was at the student center, it was vibrant most of the times, there were pool tables, businesses selling all kinds of merchandize, most of them owned by student entrepreneurs who went on to become rich businessmen when others went in search of jobs. Some bought cars as students which still is a rare occurrence in a third world country; there were lecturers who didn't own cars after years of working.

My brother had started a fruits parlour; we served sliced fruits' pieces especially pineapples, whole fruits like oranges and mangoes, fresh juice and salad. No one provided fruits desserts within the campus and he had noticed the gap. The location was just outside the main student owned restaurant, some ate fruits before they ate lunch others after the meals. It was strategic and this was a good income for my brother's family. I was supposed to be paid every end of the week but I regularly never got the salary due to discrepancies in the accounts, I brought in less money than the stock I carried. I swear I tried not to have any money shortage in the account but they came more often than not. I didn't get bothered since I paid no bills. This business attracted those who had money to spare and those brought up with class to value good diet. Some students would flatly say that they couldn't buy what was falling off the trees at their homes, their money ironically bought cigarettes and cheap alcohol, not all men but the ignorant ones. The country group produced the serious born again Christians in the campus.

With time I had student friends who were daily customers; some even came to help me sell as they passed time between classes or on Saturdays, I would visit some hostel rooms on Sundays: my day off to watch a movie or just hanging out.   Having a girl friend mostly for the first time was a big deal within the campus. I liked some girls but I didn't have the guts to approach them like that, girls were my major customers, what most men used for cigarettes and alcohol; ladies used it for fruits and sugary stuff; different priorities. I was okay with them being customers though one of them called Angie got my head twisted, she tipped the balance I had maintained of professionalism in the business. She would leave me hyperventilating after buying fruits. She was a hard nut to crack even to her fellow students. And I mean young red blooded men students worth their salt socially and financially per the status quo of the day. She came from rich parents so there was nothing you could buy for her that she couldn't buy for herself and a better one for that matter; it was hard to impress her with gifts. You would be lucky if she accepted your gift in the first place. Why I had to like such a girl from every other remains a mystery.

After holidays some guys and ladies would come to say hi and buy fruits, some genuinely felt that they had a friend in me, Nancy for instance came to say hi, she was a nice quiet girl; ten metres away she had passed some four senior male students seated on a wooden bench who had admired her secretly; they just watched her pass by without a word. By the time she reached me I was looking away, I had not recognized her due to the cap she was wearing; I was seated on a concrete bench just next to the stall, chatting with another boy employed to sell in a milk bar just nearby. I felt someone tap my back, I turned and I saw Nancy looking at me with a wide smile, I stood up and we hugged tightly, she was one of the best friendships one could have, she kept supplying me with novels, she was in the literature class. We talked for some minutes and then she left. One of the seated dudes that she passed later came to me, he knew me by name even when I was in high school; he was my brother's friend. 'How dare you grab Nancy like that in our watch?' he was joking of course but I knew he wished that he was the one doing it. I also knew that jokes are more than fifty percent what's in the heart, so he was jealous.

You know whose hug I could have begged for? it was for Angie. Angie was dark with that rich dark grape like colour, she was slightly taller than medium height and she was slim and slightly curvy. She walked with fast focused and strong steps of a confident person. Her eyes were sharp and intelligent, talked less, many times she would just point at what she wanted, pay off and leave. She got my heart pounding every damn day, I wanted an island just for both of us and we wouldn't need anything or anyone else in this world; just me and Angie, funny when I think of it now.

One guy found her buying and talked to her in a familiar way so when she left I told him how I felt about her, he unequivocally told me, 'don't dare waste your time bro, save your little heart from a heart break, she will tear it apart and step on it with a smile, if you go to her hostel room and get even a cup of coffee as a male friend, count yourself the man' he said. This was a guy I could give credit with his girls' opinions, he was a lover boy 'that girl brought Eric close to suicide; he was clinically depressed not attending classes when she refused to be his girl and Eric has loaded pockets, he was crazy about her, he offered her a trip to the coast all paid for but she refused, you know she comes from a rich family?' I didn't know by then, 'are you serious?' I was shocked. She looked classy but simple so I thought she had developed that in the campus. 'She is the only girl I know in this campus from the hillside neighborhood, I believe you know the mansions in that neighborhood' I had an idea. 'This to her is giving back to society' he said pointing at the fruits; obviously undermining my stall. That guy unintentionally did a lot of harm to me that day. I was better when I didn't know more about her.

I don't give up based on people's opinions naturally but what I heard did its job to make me feel inferior to her but I had to deal with it, the worst I could get from her is a no, right? So one day in my Juvenile bravado I told a friend to take me to her Old Hall hostel room, it was

Sunday evening, I had come to know her hostel room by coincidence. One day I saw her best friend whom I believed shared the room outside the window talking to some one inside then she was handed over something and I connected they must have lived in that room. That was the hostel closest to the fruits stall although one had to go round for the main entrance; only the windows faced student centre side separated by thirty metres of grass lawn. She could literally see me through the window of her room.

My heart pounded hard as my friend knocked on the door, it was very quiet inside, not even the stereo was on, they were busy reading I assumed, we heard some movements inside and guess what? My friend- Tupac as we called him stood against the wall totally hidden from sight. He was just around my age or one year younger, he had dropped out of high school after just one year, he was a handsome guy very light skinned boy whose smile gave him dimples like a girl but his quick temper alerted someone that his character was anything but girlish. He had started on odd jobs and never went back to school. This Tupac idolized the real late rapper who had died by the time but he was still worshipped by some young men, this particular guy ritually memorized his songs so he was given the name.

He made a name for himself in the dancing clubs, on many occasions the DJs would play Tupac's music but just in case it was not in the line up he would have one played. As it played he would make sure he is standing on a higher spot then he would rap along holding an imaginable microphone as the people watched. He would have a bandana tied around his head, baggy top and heavily sagged trousers, guys would clap at him after rapping and this made his world. On daily basis though he worked in a restaurant as a waiter; same restaurant that was next to the fruits stall.

It was Angie who opened the door, she looked at me with such a stone face without blinking; I think I read her lips go 'what the hell?' she did not even answer to my greetings. There was no way I was going to make a fool out of myself. I peeped directly inside and her roomie looked at me and smiled. She had an idea of the effects Angie had on me, how she made me uncomfortable when buying fruits. 'I think……' my voice was lost and I was sweating 'I think I am in the wrong room, where is number forty five?' I said avoiding her stern eyes; how dumb was that? The room's number was clearly written on top of the door. She knew I was the kid who sold her fruits; she was a senior who knew exactly where to put me. She pointed ahead without a word clicked her mouth and shut the door. I was ready to use the bathroom after that ordeal, my stomach rumbled uncomfortably. I learnt that the worst from her wasn't a 'no.'

That was emotionally agonizing more than I can explain with words, I never had such an experience before and I don't expect it ever again; I swore that one day before that semester was over I would take coffee in that room even if it meant sneaking in when she was outside; hell, I was ready to go crazy to make a point, I wanted to desperately befriend the roommate to get an excuse of entering that room. Although I was happy with my job I was also ignorant of social classes and how money divided humans across social lines, I was beginning to learn. 'She can't treat me like that, damn it! She knows exactly how to bring me to my knees, I have never known such humiliation even existed, I feel sick, she ain't that special; can't she just understand me……?' I lamented to

Tupac who was laughing uncontrollably all the way to the gate of the hostels.

He was a womanizer himself but I knew his type. It was the common sluts that would take cheap alcohol and wonder in the morning why they were naked in a strange room. More often than not they would arrive in his house totally blacked out. His mother- a single mum was a subordinate worker in the university so they lived in the university compound at the time and the son's behaviour was making her sick.

On the Valentine's Day which was the week that followed, I sent a red rose flower to Angie's room without a signed card. As coincidence would have it, three days later a friend of her roomie was visiting them, I just over heard him mentioning the room number on Sunday evening just as I wanted to go out of campus, I had come to play pool table, and I knew the guy well so I asked if I could accompany him, he didn't mind. Their friendship was casual; he used to play scramble with Damaris the roommate. Angie looked at me sternly and suspiciously once I walked closely behind their visitor through the door, she had seen my body language; she knew that I liked her but she couldn't even get it to her head what she would do with someone like me, maybe whip around on the butts for fun in front of a cheering audience. I looked at her briefly, waved and smiled like a Cheshire cat and then behaved as if I wasn't there for her.

She didn't wave back but I expected that, she looked at me long to warn me just in case I had bull shit in my mind I should take it else where. Her roommate took out the scramble game for them to play. I wasn't to play according to them; I was supposed to be the snoopy ignorant big boy spectator who sold fruits. I think for once Angie scanned my clothes; I was dressed quite well, a white adidas hoodie with navy blue stripes, navy blue jeans and white Nike air Jordan shoes that I had just bought from a broke student on installments, I had a white cap on still with adidas label. That was a trendy casual urban dressing, even the students had told me that I was cool looking.

I took one rack and tiles and said that I wanted to be part of the game. 'Do you know how to play scramble, really play as in make words that exist?' Dama the roommate asked with a touch of contempt in her voice 'No but I don't think its rocket science' I said being sarcastic and with a big smile. Angie seemed to find that funny she let her lips smile just for a sec. Dama didn't even sense the sarcasm which I found odd, 'we wont train you just get that' she said almost unable to hide her agitation. A few minutes into the game they were surprised that I did not only know how to play but I was good at it. After thirty minutes we had relaxed and even Angie could contribute to our conversations. It was three to four days after the Valentine's Day and I realized the rose was in the glass. I looked at it and asked how comes it didn't wither. Angie told me she knew how to keep it fresh for long. Dama said, 'some one sent without a card so maybe he will come before it is dry to claim responsibility, that secrecy isn't good for such a season '. She said 'how do you know that he hasn't come' I asked with a sly smile.

There was some silence all looking at me then Angie with some excitement stood from her chair and came closer to me, she was on a different table playing a game on her cell phone which by then was the most recent electronic gadget for the chosen few in the campus, 'You mean you know the sender? You better start talking'. She had realized that I had word power in the game and I was doing well in the game actually surprising the room mate, they were university students while I was to join them later in the year but they just knew me as the fruits stall teenager. Students looked at non students as losers in life without a worthy future. These had classified me already apparently, they didn't know me but they were learning slowly. When Angie learned that I was to join the same campus in a matter of months she looked impressed. She had laughed when I said the meaning or spelling of some words when they were about to use the dictionary for confirmation. I read a lot of novels on school holidays and between selling fruits so I had kept on checking the meanings of unfamiliar words. 'How do we spell the word referral' that guy asked himself aloud. 'Double r' I said 'how do you know that was the problem?' he was curious 'because that can only be the problem.' I said, 'This boy is good' he said nodding his head.

'Who sent it? Angie asked, 'these flowers were sold from your stall I remember seeing them, you must know who sent it or a suspicious buyer' she inquired, 'I forgot, there were many buyers but coffee jogs my memory, do you have some?' I asked with a grin that made my heart merry. I was normally confident around people without the spell of fear she had cast on me, I must have been handsome too; girls hit on me at the stall all the time, I couldn't trust their intentions though; some were free loaders who wanted fruits daily or hoping for some cash. Some hit on me as a young handsome pup that wouldn't hurt them as some boyfriends did without the slightest shed of remorse but I could never get into the trap. Some came and shared their relationship predicaments, one girl told me how she was suffering after a break up and she was only eating fruits and as she passed by the campus eatery and she saw the ex boyfriend eating a lot of food laughing with friends as if there was no heart break on his side. What was I to do? I wanted her to buy fruits but I also wanted her to move on and forget the jerk.

'What the hell?' Angie gave me such a stare but I stared right back, 'Anyway I was to make myself coffee, white or black?' Angie asked as she set the electric jug boiling. I noticed it's the same thing she said previously. 'White for me' I said not believing that this was Angie asking my preference for coffee. We continued with the game and I was on the winning streak, Dama always won when they played with Angie or with this guy so when Angie realized that I was winning, she came and stood by my side, as I sipped coffee. It was no ordinary coffee, as I said her parents were rich living in the best neighborhood in the city thirty kilometers away, she didn't even use the university mattress, she brought hers a bigger and a quality one with feather pillows, she got the best everything from the market and this coffee was no different with powder milk; the outcome was awesome.

This wasn't happening; the rich fragrance emanating from her wasn't from cheap nose stinging perfumes, the closeness! I was just over the moon; I rubbed my head over her belly slightly and she rubbed my head absent mindedly. It was such an excellent evening for me. I won the game totally frustrating Dama who had apparently never lost in the game. She was good but you see I had learnt the game with street smartness, we used to place money on the winner so making points was paramount than making words. She swore that we would play with me again soon and that would mean me coming back to the room; all was good, no! Everything was great. Where is that guy who said that I can't get coffee from Angie's room? He should see who is patting my head smiling, duuuude! This was indescribable, the whole world should know that am not hanging out with freaks or country girls who had no taste in clothes or scavengers or broke wannabe girls; I was hanging out with the one and only; Angie.

'Away with the game, congrats and enough of your memory jogging crap, you wanted coffee and there it is, who sent this flower?' Angie asked. Well, this caught me off guard; the honeymoon was over very quickly. I could see the seriousness on her face that she needed an answer, 'ummmm.....its some one you know but he was too shy, it's not the type of guy that you can call a typical potential boyfriend but he is head over heels for you, he would die for you, he can take a bullet for you while smiling, you make him shiver while the weather is hot...' 'He told you all that?' Angie asked and I realized that I was over selling it. 'He is younger, handsome, not a student yet, operates a business, and he plays well in the game of word power.....' Dama connected first. 'No way' she said. I lifted my shoulders and said 'what would you do if it were you?'

Angie was still slow on that, she was in denial; actually I wasn't in the picture yet. 'Just say the name.' she demanded 'It was him, I should have guessed' Dama said pointing at me; her mouth remained open in astonishment. 'Him who? This nappy head here? You are dead' she said going for my neck. 'If I die in your hands I would arrive to heaven smiling; trust me.' I said. For once she gave me a long smiley look, almost admiring me, she took out the card that she had put next to the flower, 'sign your name here, I dare you, sign your name if you sent it' I did it and she could see the handwriting that wrote "from your Valentine" resembled, she observed how the letters cut in the hand writing and she asked me to write on a different paper the same words, she knew without a doubt that it was me.

'Thanks, I like the fact that someone got a flower in this room but I couldn't think it was you in a million years, you have a crush on me, a baby crush that I can't take seriously but you got guts and that's something, she is my witness' she said pointing at Dama 'I don't play these games with hormone driven immature men leave alone boys, yes I said it' she stressed when she saw the shock on my face 'the ones that I have given half a chance are very few and they disappointed badly, my bar is very high and am not changing it for anyone' she was reprimanding me but still amused that in all the population of men I was the only one who took the bold step.

'Should I apologize?' I asked.

'Yes, I mean not really but you don't do it next time'

'I did it because in this entire world only you make me feel like that'

'Like what? You are funny and crazy, especially crazy. I make you feel nothing from today onwards, am a normal lady just like others; maybe with a little class' she said pushing her hair in pride but playfully. We laughed it off and the seriousness she tried to put through got diluted. It was a very funny moment for all in the room. 'And I like the fruits that you sell; that business was a very thoughtful idea'

'How old are you?'

'Turned eighteen'

'I left that age almost three years ago, if you were at least my age I can consider a date, maybe not but we would have a starting point, you sell me fruits period, and you are the boy who rides a noisy junk of a bicycle, maybe you need to buy a better bicycle from fruits proceeds, I hear it from my room every night as you go home, repair your bicycle first, right? And stay very far from me' 'I have a nice mountain bicycle I just don't come with it to work' I defended myself. 'I think I saw you with it one Sunday through the window but I thought it was borrowed, you came to show it off, didn't you? You obviously can't help it? I saw the stunts you did with it, I felt tempted to come ask for a ride but me and you cannot be seen together in public, I also saw you do something nice with the basketball, I have always liked ballers, not you of course but now I understand your preference for the air Jordan shoes, they are very nice, you look smart but there are boundaries that must be kept here, as mysterious as you are, stay out of my life' the guy whom I followed to this room was totally amused, he had no idea why I wanted to go with him.

He knew Angie was a no go zone and he was not even interested to try, he represented a group of many men who thought a relationship is like mortgaging their lives financially and emotionally. Later as a student I realized there were many of the same thought than I had previously thought within the university.

We stood up to go, Dama rose to walk us out, 'remember to stay the hell away from me' Angie told me, she wasn't angry when she said it so I knew she was still amused by the whole thing. 'Come see us off, for fresh air and the night is clear I can show you my favorite stars' I told Angie. We all never expected her just to stand up and come out but she did it without a word. She was wearing a full neck sweater that had long sleeves that she let hang to cover her palms, she had a flowered dress and on her feet she had thick socks on, this was a highland climate that sometimes became cold especially in the evenings through the night.

We somehow coupled as we walked along verandah outside the rooms towards the common entrance; Dama and her friend were ahead of us as we followed behind and I had an extra spring in my step. This hostel was like rectangle with one common gate on the southern side; in the middle were hanging lines and a very well manicured lawn. I wished that we could meet many girls who knew me but I hardly met any, I however met one who looked twice at me and Angie and totally wondered what was happening, she was the popular out spoken type, she sporadically bought fruits from me and she was two rooms away so she must have seen the cars that brought Angie to the campus. Apparently she lived in the room that I had pretended to visit on that torment day.

She said hi and we replied as we moved on, 'was she the one you visited when you came knocking the other day?' Angie asked as a matter of fact. 'I was coming to visit you but I had to fake something when you gave me that mean look' I said and we laughed about it. 'Dama was right then but there was no way I could believe it so I gave you the benefit of doubt, aren't you something else?' Angie said 'see me over what? How did you know my room to start with stalker?' 'It was not hard for a willing heart' I simply replied. The memory of that day was still fresh; I had had diarrhoea for two days just because of the cold treatment she gave me and I couldn't tell her, it was better forgotten.

After the main entrance that guy hugged Dama and came to hug Angie, just a simple friendly hug that was very common among students, I played a fool and went to hug Dama and she responded with a smile, she was short light skinned girl, hugging her was like hugging a child. I came for the same from Angie who already knew what I would do next, she stood looking at me with arms akimbo daring me to try, 'come on, for the love of God be fair' I begged ' Why should I?' you are a snoopy boy and now I know you are a stalker' 'come on! You know better' I pleaded 'just this once and its only that I am in a good mood, ok come to mama' she said with a smile as she opened her arms, I hugged her tighter and longer as she moved me side to side like a baby 'I cant believe am doing this, today you have made me cross boundaries, you are a bad influence, enough!, that's enough young fella' she said and walked off in quick step after releasing me. 'Don't look at me as I walk away, I don't trust your manners' we were left laughing 'I will try' I said and turned to go just as Dama asked me 'what did you do to my friend, she is in a rare mood.'

Dama never waited until Sunday, by Wednesday afternoon, she came over with the scramble and a bottle of water to keep her hydrated, funny that she would do that looking back now. Many girls would shy off plating a game from a fruits guy who already showed prowess in the game before, what if people gather and see you get defeated? but since it was Angie that I fancied, this felt normal, we got other guys join in and I won again though I came to realize that the actual spelling of the last word was not correct, the one who sensed that it was not right, it needed an extra letter did not know how to argue his case so he just walked away, it was not a common word, I checked for the right spelling to be sure and he was right. I wanted the game to end; they were over crowding the business space.

Angie had come for fruits the following day and though she said almost nothing there was no tension, she wanted a piece of pineapple 'Choose for me the best one' she had said and I did it with a smile. She took a bite, nodded and left. On the following Sunday I went into their room and its Dama who answered the door, she was not sure if I would go after we played on Wed, Angie was seated on her bed with feet curled up and with her back against a pillow. She had headphones on but when I entered she removed them and let them hang on the neck, 'hi gorgeous' I said and went for the chair. She smiled widely without reservation as our eyes locked briefly, Dama laughed expecting Angie to stop me on my tracks but she didn't. 'I am jealous' Dama said, 'No one has ever called me that, not even close' 'you are gor..........' I started to say but Angie interrupted. 'Shut up that was for me, if you say it to everyone I wouldn't believe that you mean it, you could have brought me a fruit now that you don't open the business today' Angie said totally changing the topic. 'My bad, will bring next time' I said. 'Will hold you to that' Angie added. So there will be a next time I told myself with a smile and I added 'I like the holding part.'

At some point she made coffee and handed me a cup. Dama never took coffee at night, it interfered with her sleep. 'Thanks, I never said last time but this coffee beats the five star hotel ones' I said feeling every bit of the taste.' 'First of all you have never been to a five star hotel but thanks' she said. I mentioned a few hotels that I had entered some just to see the inside and others for a soda but she told me they were not beyond three stars. After the game which I easily won; they both stood to see me out all the way to the gate, I never begged for a hug; it came naturally 'don't get used to this, am spoiling you, good night' she said 'just do me a favor, I must not appear in your wet dreams, teenager' Angie said, 'so today I can watch you go?' I asked. 'Of course not; you thought it was a time limited thing? It's to infinity.' Angie said as she walked twisting as if to mock me with a show of her cat walk, after a few steps she turned and said, 'stop it' I burst out laughing. The most serious girl I knew was becoming very playful.

My working bicycle that I called jingles due to noises it made was old and had many issues; it never needed a bell, the noises were enough. I was the only one who could ride it, we understood each other. It was too hard, breaks never worked most of the times and the chain came off often unless you do a pedal rotation at certain speed timing within the rotation that I had learned with time.

Twice I gave some guys the bike to rush somewhere and warned them but they couldn't hear it, the first guy came back sweating and said, 'I wish I just walked, this bicycle is terrible, I have returned that chain ten times in the last one hour.' The other guy brushed off when I told him that the bicycle will be problematic; he thought that I was just being mean. Well when he came back, he looked troubled, he didn't know what was wrong with the bicycle; it was so hard on his legs even on flat ground. You see when coming to the stall I pushed it all the way with the fruit load at the back. On the way back it was mostly a slope and a dangerous one when the bicycle didn't have breaks so I didn't care when the peddling was hard.

'Are you a magician? One needs to be paid for riding this crappy bicycle, sell it as a scrap' he said putting it down roughly without thanking me. I never expected him to be thankful, it wasn't his nature but I was alright with him being punished for his prior arrogance and pride. Ngash as we called him would borrow some money from you and when you ask for it back he would embarrass you, he would say how such money was too little to ask back; he was brought up pampered by his single mother who worked at the university. He had very beautiful sisters, two of them and they were untouchable, they lived in the university staff houses and left for the city after school only to visit once in a while.

University staff was in two categories and so were their kids, you could easily identify them, some would cross the barrier but most did not. There was the upper class that was made of lecturers and senior management and their houses were big in big affluent compounds, their kids drove their parents' cars, they all dressed well and they attended good schools and most of them joined the universities locally and abroad.

The other category was junior workers' kids; they lived in small houses far off the senior staff housing. They were next to each other making a ghetto like settlements; the kids were rough, not well dressed. STIs and smoking weed were rampant with them. They went to lower cadre of schools, hardly went to colleges. Their dressing was deliberately very provocative for girls and some were no short of sluts. Their boys wore a bit ragged cheap clothing, the distinguishing difference though was not on the outside, it is what came from inside, how they walked, talked, their confidence, the inner glow. You could tell who was who as they walked out of that university gate. Later all subordinate workers were moved out of the university housing maybe to clean up the compound. The houses were turned into hostels. It was more of haves and have nots or a caste system. Of course the decision was made by the senior staff that sat in the senate.

If a young man talked of soccer and reggae music mostly he was from the lower class of workers, reggae had words that condoned misery like 'born to suffer'. If one talked of hip hop music and carried a basketball, went to swimming pool or to play tennis then he came from the upper class and as I said it was easy to identify who was who even before they did all that, some kids loved soccer though they came from the upper class. The aura and the confidence, the body language one portrayed said much. At the time American street style was copied by the upper class, they watched it on their coloured Tvs, we didn't know it reflected of gangsta hood life and street ligalia, reckless living, crime and all the social ills.

Employees also even if walking you could tell who has a better salary, some always looked differently even walked around with a different class. There was this lecturer who was always with guys that never finished high school. One sold shoes around but his wife was a secretary in a certain office in the campus, others were junior workers who smoked and took alcohol like him. There was a lawn maintenance man who reported to work in a suit and a tie to confuse his neighbors. I don't think they bought it since he lived in very low rent single rooms. One day he was doing the lawn near my stall and the dew got into his shoes, the soles of his cheap shoe had cut. He removed the shoes and his badly worn out stinking socks and he spread them over one flower to dry. Every one who passed near wondered what smelled like that. He was fighting within, to look like a professional and his real story. Earning less didn't mean living small. One simple driver in the university had so many rental rooms and a big business out of campus.

Ngash although the mother wasn't from the top of the food chain he identified closely with them, he wasn't from the lower class either, he was from a small middle group that was made of head cateresses, top nurses, clinical officers and other professional office jobs like accountants, their houses were better with small compounds and a little bit spaced from each other, the senior staff houses were big four bedrooms with a garden and a servant quarters; neighbors metres away. The new younger ones were in nice modern apartments that were developed with increased teaching staff.

By the time Ngash was seventeen he was tall dark and very handsome. He was in high school but he behaved like a college student. Too bad he never even passed his exams to join college. He had very smooth English so he could easily disguise himself as a university student, he grew up in the environment so he copied a lot.

He had befriended June a sophomore girl and she fell head over heels for him, she found him mysterious, he never invited her to his hostel room and he was completely unavailable in the week days. His deception did not last long; his school bus brought him all the way to the common dropping point for all the high school students that attended the same school, just next to the university sanatorium. One evening June was coming from a lecture on a Friday, it was usually the day they met after almost a whole week. June had missed him so much and she couldn't wait for them to meet up later in the evening. 'I want to meet this mysterious guy' her friend said, 'whoever makes you smile like that must be damn good, I am jealous, no guy seems to be interested in me, what is wrong with me?'. 'Nothing is wrong with you, be patient, I was wondering the same until I got lucky with a rare gem. He is good and mysterious and rare, I guess he takes his studies very seriously unlike these guys who start calling on you from Tuesday' she said very excited.

He is such a gentleman, romantic, smells nice, a rare perfume I would say, too perfect to be true but he is true. A few metres away a bus pulled up and noisy boys and girls with high school uniforms started walking out. 'I see his ghost everywhere I guess, like that tall boy who alighted from the bus reminds me of him' she explained excitedly. The ghost became a human; Ngash walked towards her and on every step he made June's heart skipped a beat. The dude was very busy talking to a high school girl who was his neighbor to notice his campus girlfriend until he was so close. 'If he is like that, then I bet he is sweet like cotton candy, I wouldn't say no to that high schooler dude if he approached me, why lie?' The other girl was saying with an edge of desperation in her voice; using her book as a fan across her face as she acted totally infatuated by Ngash.

They came face to face with June; he waved casually and walked on while June looked like she had had a heart attack her friend waved back with a smile. 'It's not him, stop stressing yourself' she said laughing at her reaction. Her legs became weak for a moment and with sheer emotional strength she breathed in deep and regained her composure somehow to say 'yea it's not him but that looks like his twin brother' she knew better.

A high school boy had broken her heart and she realized he was mysterious due to his school schedule. 'That bastard, that hot looking, sweet smelling, romantic smooth bastard crushed me like a vermin, I got played by a teenager? I will kill him slowly with a smile and then kill him the second time even slower; do I even know his real name? I don't trust anyone now, I hate everyone.' she said it over and over once she was in her room. Hot tears were rolling down her cheeks once in the room. It was true his name was a fake but it was coined from his real name; she felt sick; she wished that she never met him early in the day since she missed time with him.

June cursed the day they met and she cursed the feelings she had towards him. There was a knock at the door before eight that evening, the knock had a familiarity and a timing; she went to the door but before she opened she noticed the cologne touching her nostrils, her heart pounded, she wiped off her messy face, perfumed a little and said 'come in'. She stood looking away from the door at the end of the room as if enjoying the activities outside her room through the window. He walked in still she never turned; he was well dressed in his characteristic style of brown leather jacket, a checkered scarf and a hat. 'What are you doing here, the show is over; you made a fool of me and succeeded' June said. 'I have to accept that for your age you are good, so good, you know how to drive a girl crazy, how to make her long for you, you know exactly what to say, its like someone taught you that after your homework, please go away and let me heal slowly.'

'I am sorry' he said ' you have every right to be mad, I couldn't go away before manning up and say it, you are too beautiful, I had to get to you; I never lied about my feelings, I swear that I love you with all my heart, you can hate me forever, I deserve it but my heart can't rest until you forgive me and you must forgive me, I never intended to hurt you', she knew that she wasn't strong to say no but she had to try look strong, 'get out please you don't lie to the people you love, I felt like a fool and if I was keen I could have seen the gaps, godamn it am such a fool, at least respect me and go' June said. He opened the door and closed as if he had left but it was a trick to make her turn and she did. He was looking at her with such loving eyes pleading with his beady eyes for forgiveness, 'I am sorry' he said after they stared at each other for long, she ran into his open arms, he pulled her into his arms and she weakly shed tears in his chest. 'I never meant to do it, it was not easy but I felt that I wouldn't have a chance if I told you that I still have some months to clear high school' 'ok forgiven, don't mention high school again or I will spank you' they both laughed at that 'just remain the mystery guy that you have been, I have heard of such kind of love but I never expected to fall madly in love with anyone, if you walk away now it will kill me and am ready to die of depression, that's what makes me wonder how I got here, I apologize to all the ladies I called stupid when they were crushed by guys they loved, now I even understand even how ladies get to suicide.' June said overcome with the love she felt for him.

Her friend visited to try her luck meeting the boy friend, he was there and he didn't disappoint; she never noticed that he was the same guy they saw earlier. Ngash became a baby daddy with his campus girlfriend one year later, she got his baby and raised her alone for one year as a student which was a very hard one on her; Ngash was a dead beat dad from the onset but she didn't expect more from him. Maybe she got her satisfaction, the baby boy was a spitting image of Ngash, of her love, maybe she wasn't satisfied as I said when it comes to matters love; it can be complicated. When he learned that she was pregnant he disappeared. Coincidentally those staff houses were being transformed into hostels so all the workers living in them had to move out.

June got a good job after college even before her graduation; her course in Food Nutrition was very marketable at the time. Her son was a darling, very sharp and good looking boy, sometimes June looked at him and shed tears, she saw the dad and the memories came back hard. 'My love' was the name she called him all the time, same thing he called the dad. Ngash on the other hand languished in lack between casual jobs; he stopped looking like the smooth well fed kid that he once was to a lean guy struggling to keep up, Karma never sleeps.

He met June in a mall, close to five years later; he could have missed her if his friend didn't mention of a boy who resembled him some steps away in the isle. He saw June and at first he wanted to hide but he was too much a player for that so he walked over. The five year old boy was curious at the guy squatting to look at him eye to eye. June who was picking some groceries holding his hand had not seen him hitherto, she instinctively turned and saw the dude studying the boy's face, she shed tears immediately. Ngash had not said a single word, he still knew how to play cool; 'For the love of God where did you go?' she asked. 'It's a long story' he said straightening up. 'Handsome boy' he added as he stroked his hair 'gorgeous mother' he said looking at her from top to bottom 'I never doubted you will be the best mum ever.' June blushed and smiled amidst her tears, the guy knew exactly what she wanted to hear, he was an epitome of the bad boy she could not tear away from. 'Where have you been all this time? Finally meet your son, do you need a DNA test?' she asked. 'It's a long story' he tried to evade again.

'Long story my foot, I have time to listen' he laughed at that. June then closed the gap and hugged him long, he wiped off her tears and he kissed her fore head. 'I don't live far, here, carry this to that cart and buy something for your son, avoid sugary things; you are coming with us to answer his questions, can I get you something in particular?' June asked. 'You bought cold juice or soda? I had come to get one.' he asked' we have lots of that in the house healthy juice and I have more here' she said. He smiled shook his head and complied to go with them. Ngash's friend was amazed by the turn of events, he had to walk alone.

Ngash helped carry her shopping into her car, 'you have a valid license?' June asked. He had and so he drove them, he was a skilled driver who drove even before the legal age. They arrived into this beautiful apartment building, they went up one floor into a well furnished house; he loved it. The space, the view of the lake behind at the distance, the big size TV, full fridge, it was more than he grew up with considering the trendy market styles that were in the house. He desperately needed her this time and she needed him not for money but for love and for her son, fate is weird. She wanted the son to have a relationship with the dad, men who became her friends walked away when they met the son and honestly she was not in love with any but this guy even when rugged and broke still drove her crazy. She wished the dad could raise his own son. He was broke and nothing was working out. The mother no longer had money to pamper a grown up; she had been retrenched from work. Ngash's son sat on his lap giving him all sorts of stories. When he heard that this rough and tough looking dude was his daddy he became excited, he brought out toys for them to play. Ngash was flowing very well with the boy; he seemed to have been close to kids' interests, he knew the jokes and pranks. This moment was priceless, June was very happy. After refreshments he talked on how he wanted to look for them once he got a stable job and he also mentioned of his mother's predicaments.

June still loved him helplessly, they were three years apart in age which didn't show, 'why don't you stay with us until you get a job, I will help you get one; you can even take a college course?' she offered. 'No, I don't want to be a bother to you guys, its embarrassing if I can't support my family.' he said trying to be a gentle man but he liked the idea. 'My love you can't be a bother to us, support is not only financial, there is emotional support, physical support and also how secure it feels with a man around. Look at him, why would you want to walk away from him? From us? I have missed you baby, we don't want to lose you again'. 'I have no clothes with me' he said lamely, 'we are going back for shopping then, you are not going anywhere and today we will make your favorite dinner, you remember that goat meat stew and chapatis you could never have enough of?' June asked. He knew good clothes; June was not in short of money so he carried some nice clothes home. After showering he changed into nice casual sweat pants and a low V neck fitting T shirt and even the son looked at him with admiration. He stayed and loved this new life; after just one week, he was glowing.

He drove her to and from work; she was very happy about that, the colleagues envied her, the tall model like young guy who came and opened her door belonged to the movies and soaps but here he was in fresh and blood. He cleaned up the apartment and cooked, he picked the kid from school sometimes though the school had transport; he was a boy scout very thorough even at home. The first day he went to pick the kid was after one week, he knew that he needed to eat well before he appeared in public; he also pumped his muscles to regain some of the lost ones. He went up to the class just before the kids left to the bus, the lady teacher looked at him wondering who he was though he looked like the boy, the boy had told every one in school that his dad was home so she connected. 'Daddy' his boy said and flew into his arms, the teacher looked with admiration as he signed the boy off, the boy really needed the dad, she prayed within her heart that every kid would grow up with both parents.

The way the boy played with him and wrestled with him on the carpeted floor at home made June the happiest woman alive. The house started having his touch and feel, you know the way you can walk into a house and instantly know that there is a man who lives there. June liked that feel, big shoes by the door, some thing on TV that can just interest a man, a man's lotion and cologne. He was tall, she never needed to step on stools to get stuff from top cabinets, she found several things fixed that she previously asked someone to do for a fee. He liked the way although not college educated, his logic was very sharp; actually his language was very smooth and he kept on straightening hers. She would come from work stressed sometimes and he would make her realize that she over reacted or there was no weight in her stress when looked from a different point of view.

She gave him capital to start a phone and their accessories business he believed would do well and it picked well, from the capital he took some money and bought an engagement ring one evening after the boy slept, he came out wearing a suit and lit candles; he chose a nice dress for her to put on. 'What's the occasion?' she asked and obliged. Once she came out he went down on one knee and proposed. She was over the moon. He decided to be wearing a ring also even before they had the wedding. The relationship that had started like a child's play ended up very differently.

One evening a slutty dressed girl appeared at their door, she was determined to know where the boyfriend disappeared to without a good bye. Someone had hinted to her where he lived and the fact that he was looking very different and he was driving a car. They were not in good terms when Ngash met June; in fact he had had enough of her drama. She wanted to go to club every weekend and get free drinks for seductive dancing, sometimes she would disappear for hours and Ngash wasn't a fool.

June opened the door and the boy was there too asking who it was, one look at the boy and she knew whose the boy was, she scanned the house and saw a big framed picture of the family and of course Ngash was happy in it. 'Hi, is Ngash around' she asked. Ngash had heard the knock and instinctively had started coming to the living room. Ngash had told her that he had a son somewhere with a girl he wished he did better with; she had expected the baby mama to be more like her not a refined classy lady. Here she had come to confront who she believed to be a sugar mummy but the lady in front of her was small bodied and young looking. Ngash came looking casual in very nice clothes, the rugged guy she knew five months before didn't seem to be the one looking at him. She immediately knew that the guy she met in a club and dated was no more. He looked at her with a furious face, 'I would appreciate if I never see you again and especially near my family, I hope that is clear' he said. She nodded tears rolling down her face 'I am sorry' she said, 'can I at least have some fare back? It's been hard, am trying to be a better person' June didn't need to know more about this situation. She knew Ngash could crash a girl, she also knew that this girl was going though a rough patch and she wanted to blame her ex for what she was going through. 'What did you expect? You will walk or hitch hike your way back' he said. June had disappeared into the bed room; she came back with some money, more than her fare. 'Here' she said handing the money to the girl. 'Baby you didn't need to do that' Ngash said. 'Thank you, you are so kind, I see why he kept talking about his family, I wish you guys well' she said amidst tears and left. 'Just for the record we were not together when we met' Ngash said. 'Its ok I didn't ask, this actually took longer than I expected, I know you can mash someone's heart into tears, you promise no one else will come here?' June said nonchalantly 'I feel for her though.' She added. He hugged June and kissed her fore head 'I swear no one else will come, am with the most important people in the world and that's all that matters.'

He became a reliable loving husband and an adorable father. When his mother learnt that she was a grandmother, she visited and couldn't believe of the resemblance, she felt like she is raising the son all over again. 'You kept this from me for this long?' she accused him 'June you have my first grandson and if you allow me I will call you my daughter, I love him and I can tell you are a good lady, I apologize for my son's behaviour and I want to believe he has learnt his lesson. Visit me anytime even without telling my son and talk to me any time'

Such success stories were far apart but once in a while a bloke who wasn't a student pretended to be one to attract an innocent and to some extent an ignorant girl. This Ngash story had been shared among us with laughter before they got married and it made some guys try their luck, many did not go far with the deception. They missed out on some information only a college student could answer.

I tried it many times as a high school student and sometimes I convinced some girls but not enough for friendship. 'Are you a student Milly asked me, I knew her as a student who resided outside the campus and she saw me out there riding the bicycle as well. 'Yes' I said smiling as a joke and waited to be caught, 'which course' 'BA' short of bachelors of arts. She was in the same department so she asked, 'do you take history class?' 'Yes' this was supposed to be the end. 'Who teaches you?' I had no idea who teaches the class. I didn't even know where they met but I knew the department. I decided to use a familiar name and then I imagined it was a lady that taught the class and guess what? I surprised myself more than her. The name fitted perfectly, I even suspected that I am telepathic, all the time I talked jokingly and she was confused at this point, 'I have never seen you in that class' she said thoughtfully 'neither have I' I said and walked away. I believe she looked around in the next class she attended and I was no where to be seen. She remained confused when later she found me within the campus attending classes.

I came to learn of girls like June and why sometimes young men kept off from such, some girls on campus grounds formed this unbreakable bond with one another that no one seemed to go past. Always together to their own detriment socially, same classes, same hostel room; I mean call one and the other answered. They seemed to protect themselves from the harsh world that never existed or maybe it did, the fact was they were consoling each other from the fears they shared. June met Ngash coincidentally while her friend had skipped a class to go to the bank. He said hi and ended up knowing her room, that semester they got neighboring rooms and half way the semester roommate would leave every Friday and come back on Monday; that meant she had a working man. I saw many others who walked like that until they graduated and they ended up not meeting many interested and interesting people, we called it the sheep syndrome following each other with no good benefit out of it. Some guys were the same but theirs was more of common interests that protection. A guy from my class tried following me up everywhere and I hated it, ho took long to get it but he did. I liked walking alone and deciding everything on my own.

There was this girl; Ruthie when I was at the fruit stall; when I was infatuated with Angie; she was suspiciously interested in me; I had spotted her as a freshman in my visits when I was in high school. I reminded her of some clothes she wore then. She assumed I was a senior student operating a business while I was just cleared high school. She wanted to know how much the business made so I did not trust her intentions but still she kept coming, she was very beautiful to give the credit where it's due, Ruthie had this Chinese like doll face in a chocolate skin but there were no feelings from me, I had none left, the feelings I had Angie had trampled on them and nursed the wounds and did it all over again. I should have confessed to Ruthie that I wasn't a student from the onset of our friendship. On some weekends I had seen her in the swimming pool and she was a good swimmer.

I said suspicious since I couldn't trust her; she never seemed to be in need of money or short of friends, why did she keep coming to say hi to me? She wasn't even shy of complimenting me when she passed by with her friends. She was in her final year, what did she see in me? I wasn't even trying to impress her.

One afternoon as she came down to the pool she noticed me ready to dive in when she was still out of the pool perimeter fence; I had not seen her, a good dive was something we treasured; we would do a very streamlined entry with hardly a splash of water, this was for a few seasoned boys, some hit the water and we laughed at them knowing so well how painful the water hit their bellies. She watched me swim and by the time I finished the lap she had walked to where I was coming to hold the rail.

I saw a shadow over me, I wiped the water off my face and I looked up to a smiling face, too close to mine. 'I didn't know that you are a good swimmer, how impressive?' she said with open admiration. It was true I grew up swimming so with time I had become good, everyone among my peers who grew within and around the university were good swimmers. Some girls like Wakanyi could embarrass you in the pool, she was too good, she grew up with brothers and maybe this influenced the prowess, also she came from the elite class of the university staff and her beauty and aura revealed it.

'I like playing in the water and its fun' I said trying not to be proud. She just smiled 'let me change and come' she walked to the changing room and came straight to me, she made young men salivate every time she came around here, she had a killer body shape and she showed it off. Some girls wrapped towels or other wrappers around their hips from the changing room, others wore bikers skin tights inside their costumes, well not Ruthie; she had no time for that, showing off was part of swimming according to her and some other bold girls. She was more of the type; if you can't take the heat get out of the kitchen.

I was sitting by the edge getting some sun with my legs still in the water; she came sat next to me. I passed my eyes slowly over her, she liked being admired but not so daringly, I was just being flirty. 'I see your big eyes all over me, shame on you', I laughed 'I can't help it' I said still looking. She pushed my head away 'not here, not now, how soon you want to enjoy the show of this great body is up to you' I knew exactly what she meant. 'Am diving in, we do twenty laps free style after I do my first two for warm up' she suggested as she stood up and I agreed. Few people could do such lengths without breaks.

We did laps beautifully to the envy of many guys especially those who ignored me at the fruit stall, they were not even my customers, they did not swim; they were spectators who stalked the pool drooling over girls like scavengers. They used to carry liquor which they took as they smoked away the weekend. 'What has that pretty girl seen in this fruits boy?' one asked in his mother tongue but I understood it. There were many guys who came to swim with their girls; the only problem was how they had categorized me. Ruthie kept hinting that she wanted to visit where I lived. After the twenty laps we were tired and needed a break, many people could not do even four laps at a go. Swimming was for those who went to national prestigious schools with swimming pools or for the lucky ones who lived near institutions of higher learning like us. Unlike today there were no living estates with swimming pools. We basked in the sun and she made sure we were so close to each other bodies touching. Why was this not Angie?

On one Friday she came at noon to the stall 'I am done with my classes until Monday afternoon, I am so free you can take me to your crib until Monday morning, I don't even need to go back for clothes.' that was so direct, it scared me but I made it light as if she was joking. I realized that some pretty girls were lonely against the common assumption. 'What about we swim first, this sun is inviting and the sky is so clear' I said and she liked the idea.

Many dudes mistrusted such girls' intentions even when they were pure and some believed that they had boyfriends already. This was a classic example of a lonely girl who looked like she got it all. 'My house isn't good enough to host, I need to go clean up first' I said when she brought up the topic in between swimming, 'do I look like I care? Shouldn't you be asking me to help you out on that?' she looked at me to read my face. 'I think I can do a good job, you will want me around more' she winked. 'You have a point, thou shall not put me into temptations' I said jokingly and dived into the water. That wasn't a yes or a no but she hoped that after the swimming session we were going one way. Ruthie believed that I was done with college and I was just doing business before the next step in life. When we went into the changing rooms I left so fast that she was left looking for me. I later told her that an emergency came up and I had to rush and by the time I got back she was already gone. She could not understand why I was rejecting offers some could only dream of. I said very little to her anyway and it was killing her.

This platonic friendship would end sooner than I had anticipated. I had thought that once I got in as a student the following semester I can give her a chance to visit then this would be simple. I didn't know which course Ruthie took, I didn't care as much, she asked little about me and assumed a lot and I did the same. Well, we ended up in the same department. In our orientation week I didn't attend it since I was very familiar with the university; I just needed the last one for the library to register for the library cards. Our files with passport photos had been given out to our various departments.

This final day for freshman orientation which was a Friday was the same day the other students reported. Ruthie had gone to the department to register for classes and she found files of freshmen joining the department piled on the desk, she started perusing as she talked with the secretary who by now was casual with the senior students. She was about to pass on to the next when she realized that one face was uncomfortably familiar. She went back and looked at it closely and read the name that was already common to her. 'I would be damned!!!' She exclaimed. 'What is it?' the secretary asked looking at what she stared at. The secretary knew me; most of them bought fruits from me. 'Oh yes this boy is joining our department, you know him from the fruit stall' she said. 'He is my friend and he can't even tell me' Ruthie said but that wasn't her real surprise.

After the library we walked to the student centre, even if one had nothing to buy from there it was a common social ground where one could just sit at the raised sitting areas and relax. I met Ruthie carrying a cup of yoghurt with a straw inside, she had obviously just bought from the shop, 'hi, congrats now that you are a fresh man' she said unnecessarily from metres away then looked at me with a sneer from shoes to the head. It meant that 'you almost got me but I got you first' there was no point wasting my breath denying. She was sure but I needed to know how. 'Now who told you that?' I asked smiling when she came near 'I saw your file in my department, I saw your passport photo, you gazing at the camera like this' she made a face which obviously was meant to make me ashamed; I felt relieved instead. Those around us had no idea what we were talking about but it was obvious we had some untold stories. In fact I wasn't even interested in any girl in that campus by the time and you will know why shortly.

We would meet severally in our department corridors and both of us were in the swimming team for our faculty so this one time made us interact the whole day in a competition, we would casually greet each other every time then after that semester she was done together with Angie. Just one time I bumped into her as she cleared with the campus just before their graduation around the junior common room. The reason I did not even ask the names of freshmen girls when every red blooded male was, is because of Nicole, an American white girl that I had met three months prior.

Angie never went to the college swimming pool though she knew how to swim, she had been in a national high school; she couldn't handle the glare of idlers around the pool. within the first month of freshman semester, there was a pool party organized by Coca Cola Company; they had offers on sodas and buns, they had loud music as students liked it, there was a big ground around the pool of green grass and there was a lone yellow acacia tree to the south of the pool while to the North were changing rooms, bathrooms and the office. Many people came to the pool though not many were swimming; only the good swimmers, the pool attendants made this clear, they never wanted the craziness that would come with managing a big crowd inside the pool. Such had happened when high school kids came visiting, by the time they came out one body was at the pool floor on the deep end. It was such a tragedy. They knew all the good swimmers because they frequented the pool, they only needed to confirm with the freshmen and most of the swimmers had already been to the pool.

Angie came and sat next to me, she just turned after I called her name as she walked by and decided to stay; I sat on a bench under the shade and there was room for one more, some girls with branded T-shirts came to ask for our orders, Angie had carried no money and so I had the privilege to buy her something, just a soft drink and a bun. Normally she wouldn't come to such a social event but she wanted some fresh air and then heard the music and curiously came to see what was happening, her plan was just walk by and move on but she didn't go anywhere else.

'How do you like your first month freshman? We haven't even met, young girls must be keeping you busy' she teased me. 'Good to see you Angie, been around, attending classes' I said 'and what else?' she asked giving that eye 'I am not interested in the young girls around here, you know me' I said with a wink, teasing her was always therapeutic to me, the fact that I could and get away with it, there were days I couldn't try. 'I don't believe you for a second, there is a glitter in your eye and am familiar with it, am sure that I did not cause it because I noticed it in your eyes when I got here' she was observant. 'And there is a reason why you haven't tried to look for me, finding me can't be hard for you stalker.' 'I never knew you wished to be found especially by me' I said sensing that she missed someone flirting with her or just appreciating her like I did. 'I don't, thanks for the reminder but I will give you my room number but you are not invited' she said.

At some point I decided to swim, I was already wearing the swimming shorts I just needed to remove the T-shirt without going back into the changing rooms. I removed the T-shirt and I removed some petroleum jelly from my back pack and without thinking about it gave Angie to help me oil my back. She casually did it, 'your back has pimples especially your shoulder areas' she said. 'Its hormonal, too much testerone, you see how I have lots of beards they grow in three days and it also bring those pimples, am a red blooded male' I said 'I am a science student I have an idea but I didn't know about the pimples coz it could be an STD or an infectious skin disease, I need to sanitize' she said mockingly; I just shook my head 'I blew up your candle, didn't I' she said and laughed, 'you are an expert in that' I said and we both laughed. What I didn't know was that the dude that told me not to dream about Angie was watching us; he had realized how easily we talked and laughed like old friends. I went to swim then came back to Angie, I was dripping with water and she warned me to stay away until I was dry, I splashed some water from my hands and she hid her face complaining like a kid to my amusement. 'You are a good swimmer, I should not be surprised that you are; you are the sporty type now that I know you more, urban sports' she said as I sat. Refreshments for both of us came and he saw me paying. Again that dude could not believe it.

Same day I had picked some photographs and they were still in the back pack, Angie noticed the thick envelope that had a photo peeking out when I went to swim, she decided to entertain her eyes and found many photos that I had just been sent from the United states, life was between digital and traditional, physical photos were still being developed. Photos were of Nicole and I. 'I am jealous, I now know where the eye sparkle is coming from, I mean when did this happen, where was I? I remember seeing a white girl at the stall one evening; she is the one, isn't she?' I nodded my head. She was curious, 'So you cheated on me?' she was playing with me but for once I felt like she had genuinely started to feel me. 'Nope, I didn't, you and me never became, I didn't even get hopes on anything beyond friendship, did she start liking me and maybe I missed it?' 'I can't say there was or wasn't but I became fond of you, tell me about her, share the excitement'. I said enough about the white girl 'she rescued me from a stalker, I should thank her' Angie had to say it to feel good.' A stalker that you will willingly give your room number, he must be a good one' I said. 'I haven't given you yet, have I?'

Weather changed abruptly; we decided to go, by this time my shorts were almost dry I had my T-shirt on. There were tents but we sat under the tree so we were not safe from the rain. As we walked up the steps to the little gate to the west of the pool it started to rain, we opened the small gate and tried to out run each other with Angie as that guy was left wondering when this friendship started. I lived off campus so when the rain subsided Angie wanted to go to her room; we were sheltering at the balcony of a building that had a restaurant, I knew the receptionist and asked for her umbrella that I could see behind her desk and promised to return. I covered Angie to her room, we took hot coffee and this time we were freer, the roommate was not around, the coffee and the rain made me sleepy. Angie had already covered her feet in the beddings and was taking the coffee in a sit up position. I had removed the shorts into a sports track pants that I had. The room was quite nice, a desk computer was at the table and by then I think less than ten people owned them in the university, they increased the following year, her room had a fluffy rag in between the two beds, there was a touch of money every where. 'I feel so sleepy' I said. 'Can I join you there or I sleep in Dama's bed?' 'You have dreams boy, why should I let you in my friend's bed or mine?' she asked but there was no emotions in the statement more like teasing. I dozed a little on the chair hanging my head back wards but I it was quite uncomfortable. 'Ok get in here I got some things to do in the kitchen but don't get too comfortable' she said and left her bed to me. There was a time this could have meant a lot but this time I even felt guilty not excitement when I lay on the bed and immediately dozed off.

Angie did her chores I believe she was doing her dishes, she had moved to a self contained room this semester. She found me fast asleep and she climbed on next to me and put on ear phones as she leaned on the pillow. She had changed into cotton white hot pants and white fluffy socks. Angie in hot pants was a sight I tried to keep my eyes off as much as I could; the legs were full and smooth. I had gone to her room many times and she was always covered or even over covered.

I woke up when my hand was slapped twice, the first time I though that I was dreaming but the second time the slap was followed by the removal of the hand. I woke up disoriented; Angie was in the same bed, in a sit up position. She seemed to like this posture. This here though could only happen in a different life time, I must be dreaming, 'your hands are all over my thighs, what are you dreaming about or pretending to dream about?' I was still confused, her thighs were exposed and my hand was on them then it started coming back. 'So it's true someone slapped my arm' 'yes I did, keep your hands to yourself' she said looking at me with a serious face. 'Sorry! They are very beautiful maybe my hands see when my eyes can't' I teased, 'I was sleeping for Pitt's sake; you just enjoyed slapping me, how long did I sleep? I asked 'or you pretended to sleep so you can grope my thighs, keep your eyes off my legs before you start drooling like a hyena' she said. I reached for my phone. 'Close to two hours, you were sweating like a pig so I uncovered you; you will wash my bed sheets' I sat up like her as the grogginess disappeared. 'First of all pigs don't even have sweat glands, secondly rain does that to me especially if am tired, that swimming drove the last nail' I said wondering what else I did while sleeping next to Angie. 'You are still a kid; I can't sleep during the day. You don't snore and you don't drool otherwise I could have kicked you out a long time ago but you turn and move a lot throwing off the beddings and getting them again' she said amused. 'That one I can't defend myself; I have woken up to look for beddings enough times' I said.

We talked a little more, the rain had stopped and I needed to take back the umbrella just incase the owner missed it. It was clear that Angie was ready to try it with me but my heart was miles away, fate is weird, what I had wished to have with Angie was being offered but I couldn't take a chance. 'Thanks Angie, I will come wash your bed sheets if you still insist but for that I need to spend the whole night first' I was joking as I put my back pack on my shoulders and I winked at her. 'The night isn't far ahead, is it? Dama is not coming back today' and she wasn't joking when she said it. We looked at each other for a long moment in full recognition of the gravity that that statement carried. Tears came to my eyes knowing very well that I could not take advantage of what she felt for me at the time yet I was crazy about her just months before and still this was Angie not a girl you would just wish away. I had tucked the feelings some how but meeting her was not good for me, I let the tear trickle without bothering to wipe. I wiped it finally and said 'Bye Angie' I walked out and looked back after some metres when I felt being watched I saw her looking at me through the window, she had a tissue to her eye. I turned and ran all the way feeling like I can kick everything and everyone along the way. I gave the umbrella and that lady looked at me and never talked, she knew something was up. She had seen me cover Angie as we walked off and now I came back with red eyes.

Dama spent the night where she had gone visiting making her night a long one, she hoped I would change my mind and go back, I almost did. I did not remember to pack my swimming shorts and Angie took and washed them and hanged to dry. When Dama came to the room she found Angie quite melancholic, she almost didn't talk. She was folding her clothes and she folded one short a little bit slowly and put it aside almost reluctantly. Dama looked at it 'whose?' she asked pointing at it. 'Can we not talk about it' Angie said. 'Not when you look like this, it is obviously having an effect on you so we better talk about it' Dama said. Angie sighed wondering if it was a good idea. 'am assuming that you washed it and for you to do it means a guy left it here, that would make me smile but you don't seem to be smiling yourself....' 'I washed it and yes that freshman left it here yesterday because it was wet from the swimming pool so it's not what you are thinking' Angie said and for once let out a smile. 'Still the owner has really affected you' Dama said.

Dama and Angie met when they ended up in the same room in their first day in campus and they always lived together ever since as best of friends. 'Which freshman do you know who would come here and leave his shorts and you even wash them, the way I know you that should not happen even in a dream but you did it for some one, someone you like or fond of. Oh my goodness, it was him. I sensed you had started liking him then he slowly kept off....'

'I have spent my life holding my ground against men, I said they are childish, arrogant, egocentric and everything else that I saw in them, I never ever imagined falling for them helplessly or worse being rejected, I never prepared for that, to make it worse am being rejected by a younger man who is charming me with his baby like character and his innocence' Angie said. She was holding the shorts again and folding it absent mindedly. 'I went for a walk and found him at the swimming pool, we talked and when it rained he borrowed an umbrella and walked me here, he was sleepy and he slept on my bed and believe me or not he declined my invitation to spend the night' Angie said. 'How is that possible? Did he say something' Dama wanted to know everything. 'Remember one time we found a white girl in the evening at his stall?' Dama nodded 'she was not there just as a customer, they are in love. I saw their photos, maybe I want him because I believe he found a better person, to prove am better or I have liked him all along and I was in denial and now I don't want to lose him but how, how can I like that boy, I mean like that?, how did I get here? shedding tears over love, damn it!' she said and wiped a tear off.

'He is real with you and even when you rejected him he never seemed hurt, he is kind hearted and brain smart and there is no arguing about his stunning looks once you go past the fruits stall boy' Dama said. 'yes he is real, he is such a good swimmer I watched him though I said little about it and remember he also plays basketball, I feel like I want to swallow him alive' at this they laughed. Talking about it was doing Angie good. 'So a white girl of all the males in the campus she ended up with him?' Dama wondered aloud. 'I think he charms many with those beady eyes and that smile but am sure he wanted you, I was even jealous. You were able to say 'no' and keep it, you know I could only have told him no for a week, if not less' Dama said and they again laughed it off. 'I didn't know you liked him like that' Angie said. 'He got to me too but he has never given me a second look and of course girl code couldn't allow me to hit on your boy but that night when you said I was making funny noises at night, it was him strangling me in a dream........' 'No way' Angie now was hysterical 'I won't ask about the other details but I guess you wanted to die in his arms hahahaha, this is killing me.' 'I can pay him to strangle me every Friday night' Dama said laughing and Angie fell to the floor with laughter. Talking about it was good after all.

I met the guy who was watching us at the pool later and he bowed to me before greetings, 'you are the man, I don't know how you did it but I saw you two at the swimming pool, much respect' he said, I laughed it off and said that we were just friends but I knew how complicated was the love life.

A week later I went for my shorts, this visit brought the feeling as bad as the first one, I was so nervous. 'Come in' some one said from inside. It was Dama who peeped to look who it was from the kitchenette, she smiled widely when she saw me; it was obvious that she knew something; I was hoping that she did not. 'Angie, a visitor' she said aloud. I was in the sitting area waiting for her to come out of the bedroom. 'You no longer miss us' Dama said accusingly 'well am here, what's for dinner?' I said with a smile, she smiled wider and looked at me longer than I had ever noticed, the look was very suggestive 'Campus is working for you, you look more refined' she said. 'What are you doing here?' I heard from the side, I turned around to face the bedroom door. Angie was there without a smile and wearing my shorts; it was dark red in colour with a black thick stripe going across it all around and a thin white stripe bordering the black and red.

'I forgot my shorts, it fits you so well, I envy the shorts' I said. It was true considering the way the shorts fitted her hips. 'I told her', Dama said, 'which shorts?' Angie asked with a sly smile and walked back into the room; that was an unspoken invitation to get in. 'You forgot nothing here' she added once I got settled on a chair. 'They are my favourite' I said and it was true, I loved the shorts, they had a white under wear like net on the inside and material was a fast dry and quality. 'So what if they are your favourite? You want them come get them off and don't touch me' she was messing with me. 'I did come for them, that's why am here' I said lamely. 'I am keeping them and wear them until they can't fit or they are worn out and am not thankful.' Angie said and it was funny to me that she would do that. She didn't even know that I would be coming so she actually enjoyed wearing them.

Dama came to the room and I told her how her roomie had refused with my shorts, 'there is nothing you will do' Angie said with audacity. 'Are you sure?' I asked already with a plan in mind. I went closer to her but not looking interested with the shorts then grabbed her both hands towards the back, 'Dama pull down the shorts' Angie tried to get out of the grip but she couldn't. Dama thought of it was a funny game and she came to remove the shorts, the shorts came down to reveal her silk expensive white under wear then she begged, 'please no, now am sure you can do something' I released her. She immediately pulled the shorts up and fastened. 'You two are crazy, you need to be checked in the sanatorium' she said shyly. 'That was price less' I said with such a wide smile that even Dama couldn't help smile back. She walked to the sitting rood and fastened the shorts then came straight to me, she held my head and licked my lips, eyes all over leaving a lot of saliva on me. I did not protest because her tongue and breath over me was a good thing. 'Now how do you like that?' she asked. 'I can't even see; your saliva isn't hygienic' I said. I fumbled for something to wipe, I opened the closest closet hoping it was hers; I grabbed the first fabric I came across and wiped my face off. 'Shame on you' Dama said and grabbed whatever I was holding. Angie laughed so hard I guessed whatever I had picked wasn't a face towel 'I hope it was her dirty laundry. We had two good hours of nice time.

I let her keep the shorts, I knew that was her way to remember me so I didn't argue, I relaxed with them for a while and we talked about many things then Angie wearing my shorts walked with me until the end of those hostels block that was made of units of two attached bedrooms that years back had been used as junior workers houses, they were the first ones to be converted to student hostels as the population grew in the campus, being with sitting rooms, kitchenette and own bathrooms they were slightly expensive and students who had the extra buck went for them.

'I feel heart broken you know' Angie said as we walked together. 'Last weekend I shed tears for the first time over a man, you shed tears too and I would guess why but I can't explain how I got to that point myself' 'am sorry, I wanted you so bad but I believed it was a pipe dream so I kept my heart always protected until I met the white girl' I said 'Now here you are and I can't reciprocate however much I like you, very ironical, it's a complicated situation.' I said 'when all is said and done, you and me will be alright, you are two months away to leave the campus, chances of ever meeting me are slim unless on purpose, I will try to stay away from this hostel' I said, 'Is that supposed to comfort me?' Angie asked. 'My head wants you far away, my heart wants to tear you apart but as you said, we will be alright, we must be.' We hugged long and this time there was no limit, she didn't care who was there to see. 'Take care, pass by any day' she finally said and left with her brisk steps. I visited them a couple of times before the semester was over. On my last visit she had a small party, all the visitors were seniors and they were all from that upper social class, most of them girls. Some were surprised when I walked in casually and Angie made space next to her. They realized that we could whisper something to one another and laugh. The shock was when it was cake cutting time she chose me to feed her, she fed me too after smearing the cream on me 'You are the youngest so you should enjoy this' she said very amused. 'I need to get something from the closet to wipe off' I said 'NOOO!' Angie and Dama said handing me over paper towels. Angie even helped to wipe me off. Every one knew we had a previous story involving the closet. Angie didn't care who knew that we were good friends, she made sure I stayed long enough actually I pretended to get some air outside and ran off.

A group of American students from the Iowa state university had visited three moths prior for an exchange program; it was the first one ever within this campus. A group of twelve students, two were black; a man and a lady the rest were whites. I was in the stall with my brother who owned the business, it was around eight in the evening and it had rained a little bit. My brother- the owner of the stall had just walked out to get something from the shop and I was removing some fruits from a shelf under the table. I saw a shadow approaching the table so I lifted my head up waiting to see a customer.

The girl in charge of their orientation was my customer and a friend; she smiled when she saw my confusion. In front of me were very unfamiliar faces, most were whites and white faces were not common around the place. I slowly lifted my body and scanned the group. Eva the girl guiding them said briefly that she was there to give them an orientation of the student centre; a girl at the back of the group looked at me with a wide smile and waved at me. I had never anyone so beautiful.

complete, today we know that they did not go anywhere, we live on their terms through our governments, they had taken our lands or so we thought, they took much more, they took our identities and self worth, they brain washed us and we are too far to go back. The colonizer found comfortable communities with well supplied lives that had no needs then within no time same people became 'poor', their houses all over sudden became traditional without furniture that they had never cared for before. Cash crops were introduced, employment and education too which made some people dumb who would otherwise lead a normal life; those who didn't attend church became sinners and pagans. Money was introduced to replace barter trade and the land that was communal became demarcated. People that needed no textile clothes or shoes became needy for them and being fashionable became a factor too. Their informal education that had helped them for centuries became useless.

For Christ sake our children are speaking in English while they don't know their mother tongues, is there more colonization beyond that? All our economic standards are compared to theirs and so are our living standards. Sometimes the information given out there is demeaning to shame our continent. Our governments became bootlickers of everything they are told by the West. Some whites have visited our country expecting to see a lion run after a zebra just next to the runway at the airport, really? I don't blame them; it's what the media shows out there. A media guy can come to a city and go to the lowest economic area to shoot there; some even go miles away into the country and claim that is part of the city. Maybe that happened one hundred years ago but the media never gave the new information on the developed cities and plush neighborhoods. Some of the people shaming Africa live in lower income zones in some of the west countries as compared to some Africans yet they just see our poverty but they don't see how investors have taken advantage, they have been pilfering our minerals.

Getting a visa to visit their countries is expensive and you can be denied to visit, just imagine just visiting and you will use your money while at it. The questions at the embassy leave you embarrassed and then you realize that some of the countries have needy people more than you would expect, there are alcoholics, prostitutes, homeless, drug addicts, lame and terminally sick, hungry, hopeless, criminals, suicidal just like back home if not worse. And guess what when they want to visit our countries, most don't need any visa, just an air ticket.

One day we picked a lady visiting our church from California, she had little information about the developed African cities. She thought at some point she will move from the big plane to a smaller one and land into a dusty airfield and then the city is some village out there in the jungle. Well the big plane landed into a modern airport. In fact from the air she was amazed by the size of the city below. I sat with her in the back seat of the car and we started talking, she had a list of the things she wanted to learn from our cultures but apparently we almost had none. You see with urbanization cultures are diluted to almost none. We go to cultural centres to learn what our fore fathers did. She was amazed how easily we talked and understood each other, the highways were full of cars belonging to Africans, some high end cars, not Lamborghinis or such but Mercedes Benz, V8 engines.....belonging to hard working middle and upper class city dwellers. Everything was written in English on bill boards and basically that evening it was a vibrant city. Black people born in Diaspora have been told how bad

Africa is to an extent of not visiting when they can afford. They would rather go to Europe rather than visit their ancestral land and see first hand how beautiful are the cultures, how beautiful is the land and wild animals in their natural habitats not locked up in the zoos.

It is not all lost though, many European pensioners come to our coastal cities every year and they find very beautiful young girls and even boys waiting for them with open arms and open palms, especially the open palms. Such girls become their wives or girl friends and they support their families back in the country side, it's a complicated twist which fate brought to our shores, we have the tropical weather which is the best in the world, this weather attracts many who escape winter from their countries, most of these are a bit elderly and when they think they are coming for weather they find love too, young love that's hard for them to refuse, the twist of it is, the girls are prostitutes but once they get one stable man they stick to him.

This social vice has at times led to young men letting go their young and beautiful wives to cash in on the older white tourists. Some ladies go and bring back money some end up loving the white men and even relocate to Europe and the whites legally adopt the kid or kids they had with the young bloke leaving the biological father broken. You see some of these elderly men back home are divorcees, some have drinking issues, weight issues, self esteem issues and many other sociological issues. Here they meet young girls in their early twenties who only care about his power to purchase material stuff. They are submissive and patient with them as long as they keep the girl well fed and well dressed, they can cook and clean without any complain, the men don't get this back home. The worst spouse out there becomes a good spouse to these daughters like girls.

I have seen some young ladies who grew up as destitute due to colonial displacement of their grand parents buy land and settle their parents from the money gained from a white son or grand son of a colonizer. The homes they build are eye catching and in a way what was supposed to kill them became a blessing in disguise. Kids raised in comfortable homes don't go prostituting which is illegal hoping to get a white man or woman; it's the poor that do it. The illegality ends with the word, no one seems to keep the law at the beautiful white sands tropical beaches. Although it is more of girls who get into this, young well muscled, dreadlocked young men end up with some old women who mostly never got married back in their countries. These men in many cases have young wives and at least one kid to feed back home and the money they get take care of that. They say if you take from Africa it will find its way back eventually. Billions of those who work in Diaspora have really made the lives of their relatives better back home so in a way, it all comes back.

Fast forward here is a white girl, extremely beautiful and I don't even know where to start. If she asked to colonize me I would have said yes. She was on a break before her senior year but we were almost the same age, the system here made students wait for almost two years before joining college wasting almost two years of learning. That night I went to sleep confused, according to me she had felt something and there was an unspoken connection between us.

Angie at the beginning had made it clear that we couldn't even be casual friends though we did become good friends. I was not guilty of falling over this girl. I could not fight with Angie's philosophy; I took her coffee didn't I? That was not the only time; I went to play again and again. Actually I went to play scramble but she took me as her guest more than my playmate. She became used to me and that was enough for me from her, she was a good respectable girl. She had done what many couldn't who had way much less financial class, this was before we met at the pool.

My bicycle's noise stopped irritating her as much, every time I went over a certain metal pipe that made the bike rubble as if it would fall apart became like a goodnight message to her. I had explained to her that the noise was the little mess from that bicycle she knew of. I explained how it was a piece of junk that was close to a death trap that refused to remain serviced no matter how many repair guys I took it to. It just had its own issues and it kept falling apart within days. I had learned how to live with it and to build legs muscles as I rode it. I asked her to touch my firm thigh muscles I had gained, I never expected her to touch but she did 'it has its benefits' she said. I have no good memories from the junk; just scary ones. One night I almost knocked down a person in the dark. It was a slope of tarmac just within the campus, it had rained that evening and there was a black out. These guys had chosen to walk on the road instead of using the foot paths that were on both sides. The rain made droplets from tree canopies linger for hours. I had not expected anyone to be on the road. They heard noises the junk made and moved away escaping by a whisker. They shouted profanities at me but I was just happy that no one got hurt. Knocking someone down that slope meant that I get injured as well or be beaten senseless.

Most nights that slope had lights so I was easily visible from far even by cars that happened to be on that road. At the end of the slope it was a right turn, technically I was supposed to turn that bend on the left side but that was impossible at a higher speed, cases of people who tried to negotiate that corner ended up crashing into the trees across the road.

There was a concrete slab separating those turning right and for those turning left. I always did the turn on the wrong side of the road. I kept praying that one day I will not meet a car turning the same corner and a crazy thing like a collision happened. That day came; I rode at a high speed down the slope as usual flying over two bumps that were close to each other. Just at the bend a bus from a college trip was turning the bend, there was no way I was going to the other side and fly into the woods that separated the tarmac from the main playing field.

The driver saw me coming and slowed down almost stopping; I passed by the side of the bus very close to it but as he negotiated the corner he had moved slightly to his right and that was my luck. I know he wondered what had just happened, if I had missed one step I would have bumped into the bus or I fall into the water collection gutter. Both of which could have resulted into a disaster. I never missed that bicycle, I don't even know where it went when I went to college and I didn't care. A few metres ahead lay the spot where a drunken student was kicked at the neck by another student and fell into the grassy trench. The victim refused to move away when these students hooted. They were four and I don't know whose car they were riding. This gave them some top of the world feeling. 'Fly over' the drunken guy said. 'Stop the car' I heard one of them from the back seat say. He was a guy I knew well, his father was a senior security at the university, he came from the neighborhood. He came out of the car and gave the drunk a fly kick at the back of the neck. The guy fell in the wet grass not knowing what hit him. I rode past them laughing with a touch of pity to the guy in the wet grass.

Some of these college drivers went for gold rush too, some would get innocent girl friends who naively believed that they were not married, if only they knew what the wives of the men would do to them, the one I knew would really had fun dragging a girl over mud by the hair every single day. The students would just enjoy free trips out of town with different classes where the drivers went.

Two days later I met the white girl, they had come together with one of her friends for some shopping. The fruit stall was at the back side of the student centre and the shop was in the front side, we bumped into each other and she waved with a smile, she said that she is coming for some fruits. She came and this time she introduced herself, 'I am Nicole from Ames Iowa.' She asked for my name and we talked for a few minutes just the normal introductory kind of talk then she left with fruits. I watched her go and once again she was like dripping honey where a helpless salivating boy waits for the over flow. She walked in small steps, her legs not thick but full in an athletic way, I knew later that she was in the basketball team. She turned instinctively before she disappeared, she found me looking at her, she waved and I waved back.

What amazed me was the fact that she remembered my face, when you meet new people of a different race you tend to find it hard to differentiate who is who; that was encouraging to me, things were looking up. Still her beauty mesmerized me; I got this excitement and positive energy once we had a conversation; I was not under tension when talking to her, I anticipated talking to her again, I was in love, every fiber in my body knew that. I would analyze that conversation over and over as if it was examinable. The student centre was one hall with extensions on both sides at the North side of the building. Young men came to play games mostly pool table, others were just spectators.

At some corner there was poker, another one dart board, still there was a table tennis towards the back after the pool tables.

Pool games tournaments were not frequent but they were everything to those who loved the game, normally one paid some money to play then the winner continues without paying again. Sometimes guys played for money and this caused pain to some students who lost money but they kept playing hoping to get the money back without success. Poker too caused some young men wonder why they were too stupid at the university level.

One evening on the opening day some students gathered at the student centre to play poker, John a third year was on luck, he kept on winning and by midnight he had made good cash but the way the other guys looked at him, he knew concluding the game wasn't an option. He had money that could pay his tuition fees for a whole year. They started another game and now it was after one o'clock; he picked his cards turned them over and stood up to stretch, the shop that was still open, 'I need to bite something, be patient, we are here till morning' he said. The shop was visible just at the end of the hall. He bought a cake and a cup of yoghurt; he brought them to where he sat. 'While I am still standing let me visit the wash room, hold this jacket for me and no one touches my dinner, you hungry hyenas' he said pointing at what he bought.

He walked slowly and although the washrooms were behind the building he acted like he was already reaching for his zipper. Once he was out of sight he broke into a run and took a direction towards lecture halls, a place no one could look for him; he then turned towards ladies hostels, turned around towards the same student centre to watch if they followed him, they had disappeared from the scene so they were searching for him in the direction they expected him to use. Someone in that group had gambled his upkeep money in one evening. John never slept in his room and went home by four the following morning and he stayed a way for close to two weeks. By the time he came back, the emotions from the guys had cooled down and he claimed to have lost the money in a drinking spree that same night. The truth was he really made good use of it by building a house back home.

Denis was supposed to go buy food as a duty of the day for his roommates; he thought that by playing one game of the pool would multiply his cash. It was a gambling match where by five to ten people playing and gambled on the out come. One game became ten games and he lost in all of them. The roommates walked towards the eatery and didn't find him; they bought food, ate in the hostel and washed the dishes. They had prepared some meat stew in the hostel; they ate all without caring for Denis. On the way to class they met him running to have lunch. 'We are not kids to be kept waiting for what we could easily get for ourselves' one said and walked on. Denis learned what he meant when he found no stew even the dishes had been washed clean.

Some guys were always around the student centre, even between classes they preferred to play a game or two, smoke or just hang around instead of going into their hostel rooms that were farther ahead. They were the rough type of guys who in a different environment didn't look like university students. They drunk almost every day and smoked cheap cigarettes all day long, the student centre to them was like a pool bar, they harassed and sometimes beat up freshman or sophomores who didn't understand who 'owned' the place. One evening I was playing a game with a guy who was unfamiliar, just another student that added to the masses, although as a student I was sometimes around the student centre, it was because I was already used to it and all the business owners knew me. The days I worked at the fruit stall opened up this to me, I knew also those who were frequent there, some had tried to cheat me when buying fruits.

These are the guys that I suspected to have broken in my outside storage when student rioted and we moved out in a hurry, there was no time to carry into the storage I had inside a restaurant cupboard. The stall was open and it only had a counter that was more of a big box was a lockable bottom; this is the one they broke the padlock and ate the fruits that I had kept inside. They never had money to buy fruits just the courage to steal. This riot never materialized so the students were not sent home.

As we played the game, both of us were to pocket the black ball but it was becoming unsuccessful, Jones whom we fondly called Jojo was a chain smoker outside the lecture halls; he was one of the regulars and notorious guys in this arena hanging around like scavengers. He was fond of me, when the black ball came towards the corner pocket where he was standing; he pulled the ball into the pocket for me to win. This is a guy who would use one shoe the whole semester, his jeans would be ragged and they would be two or three, he would have almost no shopping in his room.

My opponent was mad, he couldn't believe what had just happened 'the ball was coming towards the pocket; didn't you see that dummy?' Jojo said when he saw the confusion on the face of my opponent and continued to puff his smoke up; the other guys who stood around all whom were a part of the club agreed that the ball was headed home, with sly smiles. The looks from these guys towards my opponent told him more than they were saying. He was about to get it; 'that's not fair' he said looking very hurt, the one in charge of the pool table could do nothing, 'I didn't see what happened'. 'So what if it's unfair?' Jojo said and started arranging the balls for a new game. Such happened to some soft guys; some would get hardened with time and in a way join the club, others like me, were in between, you play a game or be a spectator with some sort of natural immunity. They knew me as a business operator and all of a sudden I was a student; that was enough confusion to them already. The operators of these businesses were my friends, from the neighborhood outside campus and stories of students selectively beaten in the dark that came once in a while started in enmity such places.

One of the pool tables belonged to my buddy Isaac, he was good in the game; this helped him to make money since he did not need to employ anyone. Isaac had not even attended high school. He came looking for a job from his village and got a cooking job. Later he got another job at the stationary and finally he decided to go his own way. When he paid for the pool table spot he was left with no money to buy the table. Although he had little education, he knew how to survive. He told some students to give him a loan payable in one week, he talked with each individually. He got enough money bought the pool and the loan was paid in three months. Later the same guy got one of the best tenders and even bought land and built his house. This is same guy who lived in a mud house without water and electricity, eventually married a college graduate. He mastered the art of getting tenders; he got educated informally to outwit some college graduates in that field.

The fruit stall was behind the building and you didn't have to go across the hall to come to the stall, one could walk around the old building that had high asbestos roof, the floor was made of wooden tiles. It was a while since the last waxing, university at the time had money issues; everything was deteriorating, though things started changing for the better in the following year. Some hostels were badly in need of repairs and repainting.

Some students at the hall would lazily gaze at you especially if you were a lady of interest to them and the life would go on, some ladies felt uncomfortable going to the centre due to that. As I mentioned there was a restaurant almost detached from the main hall at the back side where I operated a fruit stall. And next to the restaurant was the gym.

The gym had its regulars, they were well muscled young men and they walked around together as a pack of wolves, some people got pounced sometimes by them due to stupidity and other times by bad luck. O.T was one big dude that towered over guys, he was at least 6 5", very black in complexion and lithe like a panther. He ate in the restaurant for free. No one could deny him food and no one dared ask for money. They tried by locking the kitchen door and refusing to serve him, it didn't go well. Actually he had eaten the first round and he needed a refill. He kicked the wooden door to the kitchen and entered.

The guys cooking ran off through the backdoor. The cashier thought that he was safe since he didn't serve the food, why should he run away. He was roughed up all the same to pass the message. By the time he was left alone his shirt was torn and buttons missing. The message was clear, those few guys ate for free; it was a jungle law they just had to abide by.

The notable gym guys were seniors by the time I was at the stall. The business tenders changed hands every year; it was a dirty and corrupt affair, most times same owners retained their businesses through corrupt means; other times some lost. The previous owner of the restaurant was a quiet light skinned guy who was a senior by the time they were sophomores. Never judge a book by its cover, he could not let anyone eat for free, one tried and he was given such a chase by a furious owner who held a knife brandishing it dangerously. He came from a tribe that is synonymous with cutting people with knives. We make fun of them that they say I will cut you after the actual cutting. He was like a badger that tries to attack even lions without regarding the imminent danger in so doing. The new management feared maybe it's because they were all in the same year in college unlike the previous one. I am glad they never tried to eat the fruits for free, they knew I was from the neighborhood and that meant that one could get clobbered outside the campus and that wouldn't be an easy case.

The Gym guys had their times of training and they were not to miss weights when they required them. One day there were many students attending the gym; some thought it was fun; these were freshmen, trying everything within the campus some liked the idea of body building and came to the gym after classes. The heavy weights came in minutes later, looked around with contorted faces and I knew something nasty gonna happen. I took gym breaks sometimes but I wasn't serious with it, this time I had walked in just for little pumping for the chest, some young freshmen were accompanied by their girlfriends to watch them train. The gym was so noisy and with the wrong type of noise.

There was always some music in the gym, one of them, not tall as OT but not a guy you would mess with looked around and hated what he saw, lean boys who looked like they fed on milk were having the weights, their girls were all giggly and some girls were already shaking hips to the music; he walked across and put off the music. He walked to the higher areas of the gym where most benches for pushing up were, pushed off one guy and climbed on the bench. He cleared his throat. 'Excuse me' he said. We all looked at him, some guys were still crying out in effort to lift their baby weights. He took some seconds for them to hear him out. 'I will say this once, if you are not lifting at least forty kilograms get the hell out of here or we will have your butts', he removed his already tight T shirt maybe to show off to cute ladies as well as show his agitation due to lack of weights to train with. He was well muscled and with smooth dark skin, the girls openly admired his chest and arms and he noted.

Many of the new guys who were making noise were below forty, ten kilos- five on each hand. The heavy weights watched them as they dropped the weights and left, quite embarrassed. 'Train before 4pm in future, girls you are invited to stay' he softly said and winked, I felt for those who had girl friends with them who chose to stay behind, they murmured but never lamented aloud. The big dudes were just four of them at the time while the lean guys were at least twenty. Still no one dared their wrath. No one could risk a punch from such arms.

These are the guys that were once jailed in off hours swoop in town and taken into a dark jail. Those inside the jail started pick pocketing them. They beat the hell out of the thieves and they screamed so loud to an extent of alerting the police on duty to go check what was up. All of the gym guys had shaved their heads clean so any time they groped and felt a head with hair what followed was a powerful punch to the same head. When the lights came on, each of the guys had someone held in their hands, they punched them before releasing; they were taken to a room by themselves. The jail thieves learned the hard way with swollen faces and loose teeth that not everyone was an easy meal. With light on they saw with blurred visions what they were dealing with.

One brown skinned, slim, tattooed freshman with short dread locks guy realized that the girlfriend remained behind in the gym and he came back for her, he should have walked quietly as if he was communicating class matters with her instead of calling her out as if he owned her. 'Lynn! Come out, now!' he shouted in anger, it was evident that the young man was controlling and he needed anger management classes that were not offered in the third world countries. He looked like he was brought up spoiled, taken to the best schools, had cash to entertain those who operated on the scanty student loan, well, that did not matter in the gym. Lynn was a beautiful, slim, tall, stylish and shapely girl- a natural model. She rose to walk out dropping her eyes in utter embarrassment; she didn't want drama in public. She was the type hypothetically speaking came from humble backgrounds but was brought up in close relatives' homes in the urban, maybe a well to do big brother or sister. This meant they were mentored into good schools, got dressed but they were reminded that this was a short lived luxury. So they passed for middle class urban but still humble.

I saw such people and in a way I fitted in that category. Such girls sometimes fell for brats with money to keep up with Joneses so to say, some benefitted financially and some socially. One of the heavy weights near the door blocked the door with his hand across, he looked at the boyfriend and told him calmly 'the girl stays' he looked at the girl with a smile and she smiled right back. 'No she can't stay, you can't tell me what to do when it comes to my girl friend, you think you own this campus?' he said shaking as if he would cry 'go sit back I will take care of him' the dude at the door said calmly and winked at her; she gladly walked back with pride, the girls within the gym cheered and clapped. The boy friend was a nitwit, he got into the gym by going under the heavily muscled arm, he was allowed in to be in the audience but he tried to pull the girl outside 'you are hurting me' Lynn said. He was picked up, thrown out across the pavement into the grass head first, he managed to use hands to shield the face, he tumbled, bit some grass like a goat and then stood up disoriented, he had a silver coating on one tooth and it had fallen off, he found it easily and picked it up.

He got the message this time and he walked away threatening to report to the campus security. He did report in fact he arrived there still full of grass on his clothes but the case was hilarious to the security guys as well, they were interested in the details of the hefty throw than his hurt feelings; they laughed it off imagining the hefty throw 'we will follow it up'; he was told. It is being followed maybe up to now.

Of all the guys torn between their campus image and who they really were was Biggie; he was brought up by his grandmother and his uncles who were doing well in the city, the mother had left him and got married while he was still small, so the uncles were like brothers to him, they dressed him well, allowed him to live in the city over the holidays but the pocket money was always in short for his campus preferred life style of the rich kids. He wanted to pass as a party guy who drinks on every weekend. He tried his best to cover his lack but it was always an uphill task, some young men with money bought food from the campus mess instead of cooking. He wanted it too but the food had to be corrupted out by the waiters for him to get a decent meal.

The waiters needed some extra money on top of their underpaid salaries. What some students did was to give them less money for food they wanted and then they would be bypass the cashier, this worked well in the rush hours when the flow was high. One evening I gave the waiter some money but he had been given by others as well, mine wasn't the meat stew which was the best you could buy. He came directly to me and gave me the beef stew; I knew he did a mistake so I moved from that table. The guy who had paid for it asked for his food and the waiter got confused, he couldn't remember me especially from a different table, I was laughing so hard I almost got caught, I took advantage of his greed.

Biggie was an expert in faking the life style, he talked of money he spent but you would never find him with the money, he made sure he is clean and well dressed, he talked and behaved very urban, he was doing one of the best courses in the campus so this made him attract girls who ended up using their money on him as he 'waited' for his money to be sent, it never came so they ran off feeling fooled. They realized they were a ticket to buy a lifestyle; he instead called them gold diggers to cover up on his tricks.

I walked out of the gym after the drama still laughing after the scene to attend to customers; these dudes knew me and they knew my brother by name and couldn't harass me. Later I saw Lynn walking with one of them; the very one who saved her, hand in hand towards his hostel, they bought fruits as they passed by the stall and I knew that one freshman had lost his girlfriend just like that. She looked very happy with the new muscled dude; she kept on feeling his biceps and triceps. All the girls that remained walked out in company of the muscles guys. Some like Lynn formed a relationship where by this guy visited she in college from his work place after graduation and I believe Lynn spent some weekends with him, for others it was just a short time fling. Lynn walked tall onwards and she even competed in the beauty pageant show and came out as a first runners up which was something. She could have been the first per beauty standards but when it came to bikini section she was reserved than her competitor. Men did not like that, this was their best part of the show; they had paid to be in the arena for this. With acclamation they said the other one won, she gave them quite a show and she seemed to enjoy the limelight as she walked around on stage as if she was in Miami Beach.

Pick up relationships happened every now and then in this environment, college relationships were fragile and very fluid; some found themselves in relationships and wondered how they got in to start with. Some had the guts to walk away, some remained for loyalty purposes. Some guys stalked girls into submission while for others it was mutual. Some girls thought they were in relationships while the men were not aware of it. Many others were a lie from the start to the break up and it was sad when one got a kid along the way.

You see some girls like Nikki the fresh man girl from the city had the sixth sense or she came tutored. She could read between the lines. Maybe she spotted the fellow freshman as he reported or it was a coincidence. Dan the classmate showed interest to her, the guy had come from money though he never bragged. Maybe she saw the car that brought him and he became a target even without his knowledge. She gave in easily and he thought that his vibes had something to do with it. Not until Nikki found another girl in his hostel room listening to the dull vibes, she attacked her so fiercely and before she knew what had happened her hair was a mess. No other girl dared to get close to Dan in his campus life, some like Nikki made sure that they finished school while pregnant what they believed was security for their future, Dan felt trapped but he was given few options or we can say he never saw other options which was a very good thing, to happily ever after.

Other girls who tried that did not know how to pull all the strings and some ended up as single mothers who had a very hard life in college. Didn't May thought she was lucky when she hooked up this guy who drove an SUV to college and return the car home? Most of the students couldn't drive. Within two months she was pregnant and the guy refused any responsibility totally frustrating May. He used on alcohol more than what we used on fees but not even a diaper did he buy for his kid who was his copy right. Years later May took the kid to the grandparents, she was done trying to make ends meet while there were rich grandparents to the boy. They took over the responsibility and can you believe it the guy came back into their lives creeping slowly as an angel until he was fully back. Better late than never then and whatever keeps the family together by all means it should happen.

Dan got himself into a cell that made him not go for what university students called gold rush, it was getting freshmen girls especially when a sophomore or on senior years. Young men and ladies alike thought that they came to study only but they soon realized studies made a small part of the college years. Social education and generally life lessons was alive in a new dimension. Fresh girls were eagerly waited by hungry men who would swear or gamble over their lives. They would give themselves ultimatums as to when they will have this girl or that girl, few escaped that ultimatum. Some got depressed in latter years when the boyfriends they dated from the senior years left without so much as a goodbye and their year mates wanted nothing from them.

This is where you would find a guy with a girl and wonder how they got together, the guy offered a shoulder to cry on, he wasn't her choice even in their nightmares but he was there emotionally to pick the broken pieces. Such slick guys were all around. They would never go after a girl in her prime per campus standards, when there was competition, no, they would be like vultures, watching from afar for the last kick and sometimes they would be classmates that bring their notes for copying or that 'guardian angle' who is always checking up on you saying you are like a sister. They would even break a thriving relationship through fabricated stories just to have a chance when the hurt girl has lowered the bar. I witnessed one firsthand when my friend had this very insecure freshman girl friend.

Harry as we called him wasn't sure of how to handle a relationship he had always been casual with girls but he fell in love with this one, she was looking like a kid who never went through high school. Now there was her classmate who could not come straight about how he felt about her. He would pretend to be passing by to say hi or discuss some notes, he was the friendly wolf that you trust and eventually he bites silently. One evening Harry went to see his girl, she wasn't excited at all, they had not quarreled but she wasn't talking. He left angry at her wondering why she was behaving in such a way. He didn't have time for nonsense, he was a red blooded male; as he walked away trying to brush her away from his mind he realized that he loved her too much, his heart was very heavy at the thought that they would not be together. He went back a week later trying to learn what happened.

There was a campus bar that just like the gym and the student centre had its regulars who 'owned' the place. Decent guys never drunk from it, girls never knew it existed apart from very few that were more of men than ladies in behavior and the company they chose.

Harry had gone to check for something, a phone number that he was directed to the bar man and he had talked to one of those girls at the counter, they shared a joke. She wanted a drink and Harry had said that it wasn't end month yet, he wasn't employed so they both laughed it off. He saw the familiar guy he found sometimes in the girlfriends room and he waved as he left. This was the same evening that Harry would later go to her hostel; this classmate dude found an opportunity to bring quarrel in their relationship.

When someone knocked at the door she went for it excited thinking it was Harry, she saw the dude and she knew he was just passing by and just being nice. She was fresh and dressed in a nice lingerie, 'hi you can't stay but it's good of you to pass by' she dismissed him. 'That's ok; did you break up with Harry? I saw him some minutes ago with a girl at the bar or he is playing you and I can't stand anyone doing that to you?

Sorry this doesn't concern me am just giving you a heads up, goodnight' the harm was already done and he knew it. When Harry came later he found a very cold girl who couldn't explain anything, she just looked away with these sad eyes. He was not ready for drama so he left feeling mad.

Harry had to know the truth so he went to see her again one week later and he decided not to be emotional but calm and take all the crap that she could throw at him until he gets the truth. She wasn't as mad this time but she still gave him those suspicious eyes. She was with her best friend Carol and although the rapport wasn't as free as before this evening they could crack jokes 'this sweet, good looking chic dumped me' Harry told Carol smiling 'and I wish I know why, I have no clue' Carol laughed shyly trying to avoid that conversation. Milly never expected this talk, she looked at Harry and rolled her eyes but since he was smiling she smiled shyly too. She loved the guy and she liked the flattery words he used but she wasn't ready to be heartbroken and stick around like a fool.

'Why are you not at the bar?' she asked after a moment, 'which bar?' 'The campus one' she said. 'I don't go into that shit hole and I hardly drink, this semester I have been there once last Friday to ask for some information from the bar tender and within a minute I was gone, it stinks of cheap cigarettes and most of those who go there don't seem to have money, they are always begging to be bought something, like that drunk girl who was at the counter that last Friday; in fact I saw your boring country classmate in there' he said. 'Why do you call him boring?' she asked. 'He wears grandpas shoes that sometimes have cow dung on them that only God knows where he interacts with cows and he never changes that brown jacket; the collar now is chocolate brown in colour. He is only allowed to stick in the bar due to his ignorant behaviour' Milly and Carol laughed uncontrollably. 'Maybe he defiles cows in those sheds in animal health department' Harry said with a chuckle 'I don't trust that nigga, he has suspect written all over him.' Carol was on the bed now laughing and throwing her legs up 'you will kill me' she said.

'Maybe you took her there for some drinks' Milly said this time not sure of the classmate's information. 'Me date Tracy, no one in their right mind can in this campus, she is an addict who forgets to bathe, she is a freeloader who unwillingly sleeps with every dude who makes her dead drunk' Harry said. Then it dawned on him 'please don't tell me that your classmate told you lies about me' she was silent. 'I cant believe it, you should first of all go see that bar then you judge me, oh hell no!! I had a stressful week because of such nonsense?' he said totally happy but also shocked that he had missed it the first time. 'Are you sure' she asked joy showing in her eyes. 'Am I sure? Come here I spank you' he got hold of her hands and pulled her into an embrace then pushed her to lie on the floor, he tickled her and she laughed uncontrollably like a baby 'no no no! Don't tickle me, anything but that' she pleaded. 'You prefer a spank, Carol pass me that cooking stick, for giving me a bad week; it's a punishment' Harry said but he was just playing.

'We need to celebrate, I will make some coffee and I am gonna punch that imbecile for lying, I doubted him and I wish I called you to ask. Good lesson, always listen to all parties before you judge' Carol the roommate said, none of the girls drank alcohol and Harry was a very casual drinker. As they took coffee and chocolate cup cakes the guy came hoping to offer a shoulder to cry on. He was hoping to get Milly very lonely on Friday evening. He showed his head with a stupid country smile he immediately shut his mouth when he saw the mood inside. 'Out of here you lying imbecile' Carol said and threw a hot cup of coffee towards him but he managed to lock the door before it touched him, he ran off, we saw him through the window running his butt off, scared that Harry would chase after him to whip it. They all laughed hysterically. 'He made me break my favorite cup; I hate people who on purpose break relationships' She said.

There were always relationship scavengers always waiting to prey on vulnerability of those who were deeply hurt. Some people just met and click it off and that was what had happened with me and Nicole. I was still excited that she remembered me and I hoped to see her soon. In the adjacent rooms of the student centre there was a salon and a barbershop, they shared the main entrance but they had a partition inside. The guys in the barbershop were my friends and when not busy I would go to comb my hair or even shave my beards with their clippers.

As I walked in I hardly looked to the salon side which was on left but Nicole's white friend saw me, they had come to the salon. Nicole needed her hair braided to feel African, to look the part 'hey banana man' she told Nicole. I also sold bananas in the stall and maybe that was the easy way to make Nicole know it was me. The lady at the salon had seen me so she called me out, I was sure by now that Nicole was in there, I could hear an American female voice, I went in and Nicole was so happy to see me, she looked at and talked to me on the mirror instead of turning around to face me, I thought that was funny and her smile was even better than the first time. She sat on a comfortable chair and I stood behind her, she was holding my arm just before elbow and I was holding hers at the same level, her warm skin on my palm was a priceless gift. All these guys around knew that we liked each other, there was no doubt about it.

By the time I was closing she was just about to get finished, I packed a few cut pineapple pieces and took to her 'for you', I said as she lifted her eyes to look at me in the mirror. 'Oh thank you, come I give you a hug' this was not happening, this was becoming the day I was created for. After the hug I just said goodnight and walked away. When I was out of sight I did a dance, I had to. 'He will sleep in those clothes' the salon girls said and they had a good laugh about it. 'It's just a hug' Nicole said. 'To you but to him, it's a heavenly touch, we have been here and he doesn't even enter to say hi, he has feelings for you' one said

She came to show me her hair the following day and we took our first photograph, this time she sat at the concrete bench that my customers used. She sat at the edge so that others could sit as they ate fruit salad and left us to continue chatting. She told me about her family, each one of the members and a little bit of her home state. It was agricultural state and I could visualize those endless farms and also the cities like DesMoines.

Many students who came to buy and found us talking freely were shocked; I was the least likely candidate for such according to them. Some were even shocked that I could hold a fluent conversation with an American, this was from the judgment one got if you were not a student at the university, I went through it with Angie and her roommate; many of them couldn't hold an fluent conversation in English as I came to realize; English was for exams to them. Some talked with heavy mother tongue accent so Nicole could not get what they were saying and I had to tell her and they couldn't hear what she was saying and it was embarrassing for them so they gave up and went away in embarrassment. I had gone to an urban high school so the language mattered a lot especially when dealing with our sister school girls, they were untouchable. We also watched lots of American movies.

By the end of our conversation I was just about to close for the day, she had been with me for two straight hours and it was fulfilling, I walked with her towards her hostel which was very different from college ones, this was posh and only meant for university guests and no one else's. The rooms were in a secluded posh compound had every amenity; uniformed security and a reception at the door, next to the swimming pool to the south but there was a chain linked fence between the two, self contained rooms with hot showers, nice double beds it was a different world. This time we hugged longer and promised to meet a day later.

I don't know the conversation that she had with herself that night or with her roommate but for a week I never saw her. I was not allowed into the hostels past a certain gate but that was a long week. I started wondering what I did wrong or even what happened to her. On one Saturday I went to the swimming pool and found her there with her friend. I said hi then I went into the water. I swam obviously showing her that I was like a fish when it came to that part. Most of the students swam at the shallow end, some who were at the deep end swam horribly, they couldn't sink but there was no smoothness in their swimming, there wasn't even a style that they could claim to know. I had come with my friend Robert and both of us were good swimmers.

We eventually came out for the sun and I went to sit with Nicole, 'hey I have missed you, where have you been?' I asked casually believing that she had just been busy. I sat down next to her and stretched my legs. She looked at me and there wasn't much of a smile from her 'you can't miss me Julian, you don't even know me, in less than two months I will be gone back home and then what happens?' she said. 'Its true I don't know you but I know what I feel, how long does it take to like someone?' she just rolled her eyes like she was looking for an answer, ' I feel like I do know you, the little you have shown me is great, you are very beautiful, kind, funny, humble, you love your family and home state which at least makes you loyal, your favorite fruit is apple but you still like pine apples, favourite colour is green, you hope to work with children after graduation since you feel over protective of them.........' by now she was smiling feeling flirted, I added a few more. 'Oh my goodness you totally described me, you mean you have been that keen?' 'Yes, I guess I even know all your family members by names' I said, 'no way' she said holding her mouth. 'I said the names as she had told me, she tried to say something then instead she came to me and hugged me for long, we were not yet dry but we didn't care, her long hair dripped lots of water on me. Her friend wasn't too happy, I could clearly see that. We were the center of attraction for some time, many jealous guys wished they were me but there were those who thought that the whole scene was funny and out of the Hollywood movies.

She lay on her towel and I asked if I could massage her back once we settled down, 'you don't have to ask twice' there was no oil but she sun cream, she enjoyed her back being pressed and massaged a little bit. 'Oh that's good; massage my calves, oh great.'

We later swam and played in the water and by the end of the day half the campus had an idea of the white girl who was dating the fruits boy. We had not gone out for a real date but this was turning out like one. Once we were tired I asked 'are you busy this evening?' 'Not really, what do you have in mind?' she asked looking at me suspiciously, 'we can meet up for coffee, there was a fancy restaurant that usually hosted the senior employees in the university but once in a while some students went for coffee dates in it, many wouldn't dare, it would be intimidating.

We met at eight and ordered for coffee, she had had her dinner and I wasn't hungry, nervous? Yes. I asked for coffee cups and although she thought that we would sit and take the coffee I had a better idea. I led her out 'let's take a walk.' She held onto my arm and used the other to sip the coffee. We walked past the lectures halls; there was a straight road without branching that ran across the university grounds. Past the back gate was still the university farm but not settled, just wheat and Rhodes grass for hay. After some distance the hostels came to an end and the road was just tall trees and lamp posts alongside the tarmac. She had not come that far, there were several guys and their girls on that road; it was synonymous with romantic walks. 95% of students had never done the walk; their definition of romance was going to dance halls in town or behind closed doors, many others had no time for anything else apart from education, they reasoned that they hardly had enough money to survive how will they entertain a girl?

Those who did the walk mostly were from the cities who took such environments as a privilege, it was something close to soap opera. As the walks in the parks that were no longer available in our cities. The public parks had become so dirty, full of the homeless and human excreta in every corner, some homeless were security menace. Later the parks have been face lifted for public use and comfort but they are still very far from taking leisure walks.

We walked all the way to the botanical garden; the garden which was perfect for picnics was closed for the night. It would be a little scary at that hour since it had less lighting, the shadows of some trees looked scary even from outside, rumours had it that a lone leopard had been spotted in the canopies but this wasn't substantiated. There were some steps that led away from the tarmac over the gutter into the side grass sidewalk that nobody seemed to use, we sat on them, I sat behind her and held her, my chin on her hair and this is how we kept warm for the longest time. A few guys walked past back and forth, some got curious when they heard her voice but no one came close, just a curious turn.

The sky was clear and the moon was just coming out, I tried to name some constellations in the sky as we learned in science class. I showed her my favourite three stars that were always in one line and equally spaced. I always looked for them every time I gazed in the sky. My interest with these stars developed when still young, every time I walked out of our house at night, I saw them just above; straight ahead. One time I travelled far with my dad and I was surprised when I saw them in the sky, I thought in my innocence that they followed us. 'You see those three stars?' 'I noticed them while very young; I even wrote a poem about them' 'You did? I want to hear it' she said excited as if it would be a master piece. 'It was just a short one and when I said it to her she was so happy. Being white is more than skin colour; it is enjoying every little thing.

A bug noisily flew to the nearest light post; hit the light bulb and fell landing on her, she freaked out but I told her that we used to tie one leg of a bug while we were growing up and the bug could not fly away. We didn't have a string but she thought fast. She cut one log hair and asked me to do it. I did it and we had some fun with it, it tried to fly many times but it was held back, she could even trick it that its on the move by running with it, this was some good fun for her.

As we sat we saw a guy and a girl coming, they would be another university couple taking a walk until they came closer and we heard the American accent, she was another of the exchange program students, she was the black American girl; they were friends with Nicole. 'Hey Tina' 'Hey she said excited, so you came out too, this is great, look at the stars' Tina said and they started their share of the African sky observation in excitement. There was this continued shrill from crickets and occasional dogs barking from a distance but as we stood there a hyrax made some noise quite close by.

They got afraid but I explained that it's just a rat like animal, totally harmless. This was a taste of the African night where the night is hardly silent. If they were in the open jungles the noises would be of many kinds day and night.

The guy with Tina was my friend, he lived in the university where his mother worked but he was in a different college. He was on vacation and he had happened to meet Tina and they had become friends. It was getting colder so we decided to walk back together. Nicole still had the bug and it had slept off a little bit. It was in her jacket pocket and it tried to fly, Tina was alarmed at the sound, Nicole removed to show her what we did to the bug and how fun it was to watch it fly. That didn't go well; when it flew towards Tina she screamed and run off. 'Please throw it away, I am scared of such bugs' she said way ahead of us. 'It's totally harmless, wait and see.' Nicole thought that she would wait but she wouldn't wait. 'No; just throw it away' Tina pleaded. 'Just have a look, I used my hair' Nicole tried once more, she was still moving away. 'Give her a chase, its good for exercise it produces some heat' I said. Nicole ran towards her holding it as it flew ahead of her. Tina screamed and ran ahead, this time it was louder and from a real scared person. Nicole threw it away as we laughed it off. From the shadows we saw some guys coming out to look at what was happening. Apparently there were more people hidden in the shadows. They realized that there was no alarm so they went back in the shadows; it was obvious why they hid in the shadows in couples. Nicole went and hugged Tina as she apologized and they walked hand in hand.

We joined at their sides and walked hand in hand, all of us very happy and wishing for this another time. We walked the girls as far as we were allowed just outside their prestigious rooms. We hugged long and then let we let go; they stood and waved until we were out of the vicinity. I did not sleep for long but when I did I had a dream. Nicole and I were walking on this green vast land and then it was on the clouds, then in the woods besides a water fall. She was sitting on the railings without fear and I kept warning her to watch out. 'Don't worry she said, I can fly like a bird, she jumped off into the falls and I trusted her word that she would fly, after all she was an American. They did everything in the movies, they were gods. And true to her words she came back flying and stood smiling in front of me. She was wet with the mist and I loved the way her hair looked when wet. 'I feel cold' can you make me a little warm?' she asked and came into my embrace. I gladly embraced her; I took out my jacket and covered her. The sun just appeared and shone on us. 'This is so beautiful and romantic' she said 'it is' I said but my voice wasn't audible. Vapour rose from her and it was a lovely sight, she turned and I embraced her from the back. 'I want to fly again' she said and walked to the edge again. She jumped off, I saw her coming but this time she never reached me, she kept being pulled off by something like a sanction in the cloudy vapour, I was in agony wondering how to pull her but she kept disappearing, it took longer every other time until she appeared and said 'I am sorry' then she never came again. I woke up confused.

We met for swimming the following day in the afternoon, the dream still bothered me but I pushed it away. I rarely dreamed and if I did I could not remember. This afternoon most guys of her American group came to the pool, actually all of them from head count. I was familiar with some of them by now, one guy called David was swimming with us, we talked a lot, he was from California and generally a cool tall dude who was genuinely interested to learn as much about Africa as possible. I took him though the Geography and also the history of the continent. They were subjects I took interest in.

David thought that slavery was from all Africa but after explaining the Geography and why it happened in the western Africa rather than East Africa and he got it. In those days there was no Suez Canal so it would be a long journey to cross from our coast round to South Africa. I realized he had little information on the American celebrities we idolized. I thought everyone in America knew the late Tupac and Snoop or at least Beyonce. He thought they were familiar but he wasn't sure what they did or how popular they were with the black community. He didn't know the songs we knew, he liked music but all the artists he knew or bands were not as popular to us as he thought they should be. At least he liked backstreet boys and they were popular in our country; if he didn't know Michael Jackson I could have been offended but he knew of him 'That is a great dancer, he turned from black to white right?' he asked as if I had an answer.

I had always thought that out there they were all like one tribe, I was so wrong; I came from a country that has forty tribes with individual dialects. I thought the language united people as one. There were some black and whites who felt closer to each other in some communities than some blacks with blacks or whites with whites. They had economic tribes, social tribes, intellectual tribes and so on. 'quite a number of guys in college had earrings, they copied the black Americans that they adored in rap music and Rand B as well as movies, we had been colonized by the black Americans in lingo, dressing, swag and to an extent vanity of today's glamour forgetting tomorrow, music, acting and in some adorable areas like entrepreneurship and talents exhibited in people like Tyler Perry, Oprah, Denzel Washington, Will Smith.........basically all the high profiled celebrities that have it together. We listen to their stories and we stop using any excuse, we talk to ourselves out of mediocrity and work hard to achieve our goals.

'Why is it common for American men put on Earrings?' I asked him. In high school some boys were asked by the principal to go home until their ear lobe holes sealed up. Nowhere in the dos and don'ts of our school had that stated, how was it even an offense? They left the boarding school and came back with bandaged ear lobes. Once they healed they left a pimple like stump on the ear. The principal couldn't understand that culture, he connected it with lawlessness. Those guys were in fact quiet and obedient boys. We learned with time that the hood style was from the ghettos not in well to do families; ironically those who adopted it here were the middle class and mostly the upper middle class, they watched movies and paid cable series.

All Americans are rich we believed so anything they did was worth emulating. 'They do it for beauty, identity, freedom....' David said and that was it; freedom was the epitome of the American culture, land of the free. They did it because they could do it; it was a culture out of freedom. That afternoon the pool was well mixed with black and white and we had fun. We had a basket ball and we played a game with it, by the time we left we didn't want to go, I asked Nicole if we could go for coffee in a restaurant just next to the swimming pool up the steps to the west. It was a classic one that had few students eating there on some occasions. The university conferences were help on the upstairs of this restaurant.

'That's a great idea, it will warm us up', 'we are going for coffee' she said aloud to her friends and we ended up going there as a group. The restaurant area was expanse and we took different tables, I picked one at the corner where we could be secluded. We were not in a hurry, we took coffee and muffins, Tina and her guy were not far off so we could talk over to each other. This restaurant had never been too noisy like this day. The manager came over and liked the life and the mood in it. So many times it was too quiet and too solemn but for around two hours we made it lively.

The following weekend we planned for a hike to some caves where a skeleton of the early man was found. It was a popular destination for hiking and goat eating. For those who wanted to go farther than the botanical garden they picked this destination far into the bushes across the river. We had a goat eating in our last Semester. Usually after exams we could do a class party but in the hostel. This one was outdoors, the goats were expensive than what we had. I had told my friends that for us to get a goat worth eating we needed more money that we didn't have. They didn't listen to me; they went shopping from the farmers outside the campus. Previously we could just buy meat and cook. I had given them an alternative; the poultry department was always culling the layers at a good price.

That money could have been given us ten chicken and that would have made a good meal. They came back totally stressed and tired; they asked me what to do. I had previously opted out of the party since I knew it would be a disaster with a baby goat for the main meal. My friends came for advice and begged me to join back. 'If you are not in the party then it's not worth it, you know that bro, you see all these other guys have no idea even where to get meat but just because they contributed they believe food will be ready and enough.' we all knew that we need you but we played hard.

They agreed to my idea, we got ready on a Saturday and by noon we were at the venue, we were already hungry and the food was hours away. As we worked on the chicken I realized that the intestines were not dirty, I told the guys that we can wash them and roast them over the fire wrapped up around sticks. Some had no idea what I was talking about but sooner than later they were salivating over the intestines, the aroma was too appealing. Up to now the girls had not joined us, we realized that we needed to move ahead and they could find us a step ahead in food preparation, we had not assigned them any work apart from gracing the party.

We heard the girls coming noisily through the thickets; we had set camp on an open area that had some wooden benches for such moments or just when you rest and commune with nature. I had walked over past the thickets and realized that we were near the university fence, there was a settlement two kilometers away and as we started fire some two guys went for the illicit brew they had taken before.

The girls came into the opening and my boys sold me out. They believed that eating intestines would make them look cheap so they walked away from the fire and some even said aloud 'roast your intestines' pointing at me, 'They are mine now that you see girls? Okay I will eat them alone, idiots', I said furious with them. 'What's ready? So hungry here', the girls asked. I was just removing the intestines from the fire into a plate. I didn't have any inferiority complex, I took the intestines and walked to a far bench 'these are mine alone' I said as I started chewing on them. 'Please let me have some' Brenda the most beautiful in the group came to me begging. I gave her a stick and the other girls followed. 'This is so yummy, you are the best' she said pecking my cheek and sitting next to me; the praises were on me. Some guys felt foolish and came for them too but they got nothing, it was a lesson to them. They really felt silly for walking out on me while they had participated in the roasting. It is funny that most of these guys had no girlfriends in the campus; they were too inferior to approach them, how was that even possible? They preferred to date less educated girls back in their homes. Now they were the same running away not to be ashamed in their last two weeks of campus by ladies who didn't care.

When the main meal came every one was getting at least one thigh and another piece of meat, we had other food to accompany the chicken.

When I was served my first thigh I picked it and asked for another, from my calculations I knew they were more than enough for everyone. I was given one more and I did my first mistake of the day, I over ate. I didn't realize it at first but as we walked back to the hostels I realized that my stomach was really stuffed. It was in the evening with little to do; I went to relax in bed as I took warm water.

Doreen came over; she was also a senior but from a different department. She was a good friend who did not need to alert me if she wanted to pop in, we watched movies together, we were so alike socially and time went fast when we were together.

If someone knocked on the door and just pushed it open, it meant that he or she was a close friend. The hostel room opened to a small living room, two bed rooms to the side and a kitchenette at one corner, same hostels that Angie lived in, in her last semester. The bathroom was outside adjacent to main door hidden in the corner. Every bedroom was normally shared by two individuals making the total hostel occupants as four. For a strange reason that Semester I found myself alone in the room. I didn't know who was to be my roommate and he never turned up.

I heard a knock and the door opened, my other two roommates in the next room were not in, we used to joke that Doreen was our forth roommate. She visited enough times, sometimes she came to study in my room even when I was not in, I had a television and she followed some programs so instead of using the common TV rooms she would come and watch from my room. Every Friday we cooked a chicken which was a delicacy and Dee as we fondly called her was always with us.

She knocked pushed the main door open and just came straight into my room which she never bothered to knock, she burst in; she had a bag of hot French fries and a soda in a khaki bag. 'What's up my nigga?' we laughed at that, it was a phrase we had picked from a movie the weekend before from Rush hour movie and she thought it was funny 'You have a mission to break the door? What if I was naked' I said, she sat on the bed next to my feet 'this cheap door can drop for all I care, for you being naked, I have been to the zoo to see your cousins and I have no plans to go back there.' I laughed but she laughed louder than me at her own joke 'what are you watching?' she asked 'Nothing important, just some boring news, waiting for something better after wards' I said. She opened her fries and started eating. 'Where is my bag of fries?' I asked jokingly. 'I am not your mother' she said and we laughed again and this is why she was always the best visitor in my room. Dee was always with a fast thought humorous answer.

'We had a class bash this afternoon, I can't even eat, I am so full I hate myself' 'you had a bash and you never invited me?' she asked punching me.

'It was a small class one so I didn't invite anyone and I had refused to attend until two days ago'

'So what if I wasn't invited, all I need is to know the place and time? I crash parties all the time without apologies and I know half your class through you; that would have been easy' she was right.

'Sorry next time' I said.

'Really? Next time indeed, you have less than two weeks in this damn place, which next time are you talking about? I am mad at you, I am glad you over ate, enjoy the discomfort' she said with a sneer. I couldn't understand why some people hated the campus; they felt it was one of their worst times while some loved it. I was very comfortable but Dee complained of several things.

'I wish I would care about that but we both know that I don't' I said smiling.

'And I hate you more for that'

'I know but there is some chicken in the kitchen you can knock yourself out.' She went for it immediately.

She came tearing it apart, 'so yummy who was the cook' she said as she pecked my cheek. That day I was getting lots of them.

'You hate me remember, men were in charge of the kitchen today' I said.

'I really wish that I could manage to hate you, I hate Nicole, we know what we could be if she wasn't in your heart, look at her, she ain't nothing but white' she said with pointing at her picture that I had on the wall of Nicole and myself.

She had a point, we were close but I couldn't let us cross the boundary, by all means she was beautiful and lively. Some people thought that we had a relationship but my close friends knew better. Dee was jealous if she found any girl in my room even if she was asking for class notes or just courtesy call. One time she found this girl in the room seated on a chair, Dee removed shoes and spread herself on the bed. That was a sign of marking the territory; the other girl did not stay long after that.

‘Leave Nicole alone, she is innocent, I met her before I met you and as much as we click, I haven’t had a closure with her.’

‘Clinging on her belittles both of us, we know better, when is that last time you got at least an email from her, again? Six months or more, come on, wake up and smell the coffee’ she said emotionally. ‘You know I love you and I can’t wait for ever but I have tried and the worst part is, I fell for you when you were not even trying to get me,’

I read this novel while in high school which was based on a love relationship in the university, I felt that I could want to end up with someone we went to university with, Dee was the closest it could get.

I met Dee in a hostel room where she had brought another girl, I just learned her name and the fact that we talked very easily. We later met outside the student centre, it was the beginning of a new semester so there was no hurry, we sat at the raised sitting concrete as we sipped on sodas, from that time we exchanged phone numbers and even hostel rooms and naturally we became very good friends. I invited her to church; the Christian union fellowship and she came regularly shocking her friends who believed church was for the corny guys. What was even amazing is that she would dress up for church in a dress.

That dream that I had of Nicole disappearing into white cloud was coming true through the emails, communication became less and this time it was like I had had the last communication, face book was just picking up and she wasn’t even on it or she used a name that I couldn’t know. Dee was on point and I was wondering what to do.

That meat wasn’t mine, it was for Vic my classmate, he was one of those who wanted to embarrass me with intestines; he was also fond of the illicit brew. After eating he took some and he came staggering. I offered to help what he was carrying lest he dropped it off on the way. He walked slowly as the effects of the alcohol that he drank in a rush got to his legs so I left him behind 'get this in my room' I said, he never came so I gave it out. 'I took that meat from Vic, he was so drunk to remember' Dee knew him well 'that drunk can't remember anything, lucky me then'

She fed me with fries, 'I am not hungry, I just missed to bite something' she said 'Girl I can't eat, I will puke on your face if you put more food in my mouth; this stomach is beyond full', I was in a vest with my stupid stomach exposed, she rubbed it 'oh poor boy, you ate like it's the last supper' we laughed and we always laughed off stuff. Dee was from a rich family, she never needed anything from anyone, she was like Angie, I don't know how I became friends with such girls and the irony was, one couldn't be with me though I badly wanted her initially and the other one wanted but I wasn't ready for it due to an entanglement with another. It was pure friendship and admiration in both cases then I would later learn of their back grounds and they were both not the bragging type.

Angie wasn't friendly but Dee was very friendly. 'I just fell for one guy who doesn't feel the same in this entire campus, or pretends not to' she reminded me. 'Life is hard all around', I said. 'I fell for a girl who is across the ocean who hasn't written to me in the longest time but I need to believe that we can have a life together'. 'Forget her, I wont beg but all I need is a go ahead and I will swallow you alive, you know I can; you can't have unfinished love chapters all your life, at least finish one' today she was bolder and what she said hit me with renewed reality.

'Can that start when my stomach isn't full?' I asked. 'You mean it?' she asked excited. 'I am a Christian so don't get funny ideas' I reminded her. That's all she needed, she meant what she said; she spent the night. We had started watching a movie and I believed she was watching only to find her totally asleep. My last two weeks of campus were filled with her presence in a different way than I could have ever imagined. She spent so much money entertaining me, I felt spoiled.

………………………………………………………

The day for the adventure into caves came. The four of us gathered with our back packs, we were well dressed for the hike, we had a seven mile walk to the caves, after the campus limits; we had to follow a murram road then after some settlement where guys bought the illicit brew branch off into the woods. We started walking towards the back gate of the campus, through the botanical garden there was a route that I knew. The fence on that side was broken and some people trespassed inside but there was little you could do, if caught from outside you would be taken to the cells and not to mention the big German shepherds that patrolled at night. As students during the day no one would really care. This route was diagonal to the one using the gate. Just after the botanical garden there was the university abattoir, sometimes before we had gone to climb the ladders to the overhead tanks, the fun was the view from that vantage point.

We waved at the guards that were at the gate, it was around ten in the morning there were no visible students but I knew they were on the way; they would come to read books under the trees in this serenity, others would come with their dates and others just for relaxation. The botanical garden had attracted many birds and this morning was no different, the American girls enjoyed looking at the birds and taking photos of them, we also took photos in there. I saw a big eagle like bird under a huge canopy of tree; I hushed every one and pointed at it. Nicole as I guessed got amazed and with the camera ready started slowly towards the bird, the bird was oblivious of her actions until she was very near. She could have reached it but she came to a depression hidden by grass. She lost her balance and fell and cursing out in the process.

The bird flew away startled, we had a good laugh then we walked on, just after one hundred metres Nicole dropped her back pack and was writhing her body. She started removing her jacket; then stamped her feet. Safari ants had crawled inside her body, the next minute she was dancing and crying out 'oh my god, oh my ....They are biting me she rushed off the trail into the bushes to go sort herself out. 'Tina come and help' she called out. Tina dropped her bag and walked behind the bush 'Oh my why are you naked?' Tina asked. 'They are every where, look' we heard Nicole say, 'help me check, this is clear and this....' We were having a good hushed laugh as we heard them talk. 'Do you need help, this is normal in Africa?' I asked jokingly 'No you boys stay out there and watch out for anyone' she said. It took a few minutes then Tina came out 'I need your help now' Nicole called out, I was confused as I walked into the clearing but she was hiding, I felt something touch my neck, I jumped in fright. 'She laughed so hard her knees buckled. Once she got control she asked, 'isn't that normal too in Africa? I guess you expected to find me naked like a buck, sorry'

'Come here I kick your butt, you really scared me, I thought it was a spider or a tree snake' she ran off and I ran after her, caught up with her, she turned and said 'keep off my butt, I wont scare you any more, you laughed at me so I had to do something too' we were all goofing. 'Slap her butt I know you want it' Tina said and they laughed. It was a nice walk. We walked out of the bushes into the open. A hundred metres away there was the fence we joined the rough road and a truck full of logs passed by. Illegal logging was rampant and indigenous and the exotic trees were fast depleting. We passed by the local centre that had wooden shanties that made the shops and eateries. 'Let me give you a taste of some food here' I said and led them towards a café. They are deep fried wheat dough that we call Mandazis. The dough is done with baking powder so it bulges, locally a fried egg is put in between and then you eat as one piece. It's heavenly, not so good for checking your weight but here we have little issues with weight. By the time we got them wrapped some kids were around curious about the white skin. They connected white colour with generosity but Nicole didn't know why they came around. She took photos of them and since I knew what they wanted, I bought sweets/candies and told Nicole to give them. They were very happy. They followed us for a kilometre just for fun. Again this was common in this kind of environment.

We were getting into the thickets going down a slope that let to the river. We bid the kids goodbye and we disappeared, we walked in a single file until we came to the river. We had to walk alongside the river for long until we came to the crossing area; there were rocks that we needed to step on to cross. Tina needed some encouragement, she was afraid that she would miss a step but she did not. 'Eat this before it gets cold. We started munching on our snacks 'this is good' Tina said 'very good' Nicole added. 'What do you call it?' Tina asked 'I need to learn how to make it' There wasn't a name specifically for it but I said 'spicy hot egg burger.' 'It's hot in many ways' I taste some pepper, I love it'

Tina said. 'This is such a treat' Nicole said, she looked at me with those eyes that showed gratitude, deeper than the mouth said. 'Stick with me and you will always eat delicacies' I said jokingly. She held my arm and leaned towards me. The narrow river bubbled just next to the trail; the air was very cool under the bushes. Birds were curious and they flew off in a panic every time we were so close, I don't believe that they felt threatened, more likely they thought it was a good game. We had to watch the low branches especially us men, we had the height.

The caves were visible, there were hanging roots almost making a door to the entrance, it was dark even from five hundred metres away, the bushes here were clear and the path wider. I believe people had cleared with more visits and goat eating. Talking of goat eating I had a distress cry from a goat, I sensed one was losing its head just outside the cave that morning. Here we walked hand in hand, the sun was bright in the sky; we had forgotten about it while in the thickets, though sweaty we liked the feeling of the sun on our faces.

Fifty meters from the cave we found two guys slaughtering a big he goat. Fire was burning nearby. They were not familiar to us and they were not students, more like the locals. Why they had chosen that spot? The goat wasn't stolen, if it was it could have been slaughtered in a hidden place and who would eat such a big goat, definitely more than two guys. This was for a bigger group. We said hi and we walked into the caves, they gave us a longer look than usual because of the white girl.

'Now remains of the early man; Kenyapithecus from your tour guide of today were found lying inside here, he lived alone or the other family moved away after he died. I believe he chose here due to security, warmth and proximity to food from these bushes like edible herbs and fruits, duikers and water, his life was of hunters and gatherers no sign of fire' I said intending to impress. I loved history so I said everything that I thought was intellectual for such a visit. 'Impressive' the girls said. Of course I was looking for such compliments.' Towards inner parts it was dark but few metres the light was enough. There were rocks to sit on and we sat to catch our breaths. We were sipping our water. Both the American girls took out their journals and updated them. We were not used to this; we kept memories and emotions in the mind and heart; never on a paper. We had taken different photos along the way and now when they were done we took more. The two guys were already cutting the meat and ready to cook. We walked around, swung with roots that hang at the entrance. We talked and shared about many things, we asked about America apart from what we knew from the movies, the real America they were slowly learning that Africa was not as dark as they described. Things were different but the same. Humans are humans. Deep down they care about the same things, they want peace, they love beauty and tranquility of nature, they ate and different food doesn't mean bad food. What was called poverty was actually a way of life. Some of these folks did not need cars or those houses. Their wealth was in the farm produce, wellness of their families and cattle. Their budgets were low so calling them poor was using parameters not meant for them.

We learnt that Americans had unmet needs and fears too. Both of these girls never came from riches but they came from comfortable families. Tina's mother was single and that meant more working hours for her mum. They were both on student loans and they dreaded to pay them once they started working. Hidden racism was still an issue in their country, divorce rates were so high and they had close people who had been affected, crime, terrorism effects after 911. They all had humanly issues just like we did. Nicole's dad was a farmer and the farm wasn't doing that well so according to their needs they needed more money. I actually sympathized with them once I removed the fact that they were from another continent from the picture. We swung with hanging roots from the top, played around for at least one hour after resting enough.

We heard a group coming, it was loud and untamed. Before they came to the opening we knew the area will be noisy for a while. Birds flew away and these guys scared them on purpose. We watched who the rowdy guys were, when they came to the opening which was wider they broke into a jog, they had the rugby ball that they started throwing it to each other. These were definitely students that we knew of, it was the rugby team. Now it made sense about the goat that was now cooking. It was their party in the bushes. They bought the goat and paid those guys to start off with cooking. They had to make an entry even if no one was seeing. More of their food was brought; I knew they had girls they were just following behind. Slowly by slowly the girls came, the whole group was charged, they must have taken the local brew or they took little alcohol along the way, these were the types that would smoke weed with their wild ladies I saw in their company.

Majority of them knew us, they were happy to see us as if we were part of the group, they hugged us and they hugged the girls, some of them unnecessarily long and tight to their discomfort especially those whose mouth smelled like an illicit brewery. Local brew with time had people doing crazy things to it to attract more customers. It was more of witchcraft thinking that I don't believe worked. When the police invaded their dens and poured out the contents; the bottom of the tank was sometimes found with women panties and in some cases rat skeletons. Some used methanol may be it was cheaper but some customers had lost their eyes in drinking spree. It was a wonder and foolhardy to continue drinking from such. In one case of blindness these men couldn't see anymore but they thought that it was lights turned off. 'We will drink even in darkness, one can't miss the mouth' little did they know that the lights were still on and they needed some hospital emergency, some had regained their eye sights some didn't.

These guys had carried even a stereo to provide music; they played music as they played a game in the open area. The girls danced and cheered, this jungle had become something that animals were not even aware of. That could have been the most awkward day for them. Meat was ready, big fried chunks. We took a piece each and left, we were not part of this crazy party. The girls had clothes to walk to the venue and then for wearing at the venue. They removed the covering clothes and remained in what was close to a hooker's street attire. They danced very provocatively, the muscled boys joined them every now and then and it was not a sight one would endure if you were not part these guys.

'Wow that was so crazy and intense' Tina said 'it reminds me of football teams back home' 'even basket ball men can do that, together with cheer leaders, isn't funny how humans have same behavior across continents. I have heard of parties in grave yards by the popular high school kids, that's creepy' Nicole added. 'Grave yards? Don was shocked. 'We stay away from grave yards in fear of ghosts' He was from the tribe by the lake side and they revered the dead. They don't even believe that one should be buried away from his birth place. They encounter great expenses to travel the bodies even from abroad. For me grave yard party isn't normal but we had little fear of the dead. One was buried where he died, especially if it's a far distance. I knew people who were buried at the coast, seven hundred kilometres away from home.

We were just about to get out into the open where we had bid the kids goodbye when we heard some shouts and commotions, some one was running and definitely there were two dogs at least. We turned and there was a duiker running for its life and two dogs in hot pursuit. When we turned it got confused and turned almost directly to the dogs, the nearest dog missed but as the duiker jumped into the thickets it got stuck in a v shaped branch. Maybe it could have pulled itself out if the dogs were not so near. One mongrel bit the thigh and started tearing off the meat. The partner arrived and started on the other, the duiker cried out in pain with eyes wide open. The hunters came and shouted for dogs to stop. The dogs were not fast to stop so the two hunters kicked them off and all these dog cries touched the American girls. 'Stop kicking the dogs, they went closer' the guys couldn't talk English so we explained what the girls were furious about. They only smiled. 'These dogs are so used to being kicked, they love it' one said

The hunting of any game was and is still illegal but when it comes to the small types of wild animals, people hunted for food without the authorities caring or noticing. The guys cut off the duiker's neck as it cried painfully kicking with its last bit of energy. They slit open the stomach quickly as experts and pulled out the whole gut which they threw to the dogs. That was the pay off for the hunt. The dogs devoured the guts hungrily even fought each other. The intestines were not cleaned but the dogs never seemed to mind. At that point I didn't know whether that made our adventure more fun of it ruined it. Both girls were in tears after this ordeal. 'Can we cut you some meat' they asked 'no we are good' we said.

They carried it off into the thickets and totally disappeared as the two dogs trotted behind. If I was alone I could have carried. Game meat was always better. I had eaten hares and gazelles, had had a bite of giraffe and zebra. All this was illegal meat hunted by people but sometimes maasais; an indigenous tribe would cut off meat from lions and that made it legal since they didn't do the killing. They would walk as a group of five courageously to the extent of scaring the lion off the meat. They would expertly cut off a hind leg and walk off with it and the lions would go back into the meat. My dad had worked in a town within the tribe so we could get wild meat every now and then from his friends.

It took sometime for Nicole to get control of herself, took even longer for Tina. 'They killed an innocent duiker and they mistreated the dogs, that is very cruel, aren't there animal rights here? I am looking for a police station to report this' Tina said. 'I forgot to take pictures, I was so traumatized; that image and sound will haunt me for days' Nicole said. 'Have you ever hunted?' she asked. I had hunted and we got nothing to carry home.

Our dogs had caught a hare and although I saw them chasing it, I didn't know they had caught it until they came back to me; both had blood around their mouths. They had greedily tore and swallowed the little thing, in only a minute they had eaten it. 'This is nothing here, to them this was a success, they have families that will celebrate the meat, its one mans loss becoming another man's gain, dogs culturally in our communities are good for security and hunting, no special treatment is given to them. They sleep outside and others spend a lifetime chained around their poop. Finding a dog in the house is a disaster for the dog. They know their place. Some don't cook for the dogs and never fed the dogs intentionally. The dogs just took care of themselves' I explained. 'The way I have seen the white guys riding with dogs in the car, not here, I love dogs myself but we are not many. I don't like the guys kicking the dogs but I have seen it so many times so it's expected especially in such bushes. Dogs are tools not companions to them'

Life does change that now we have dogs in the houses and also we ride with them in cars mostly for the imported pet dogs, the life that's thought exotic slowly creeps into our lives in the cities and realize the love some people have for animals and especially their pets.

This could not settle in them. We came to the shanties again, walked and waved to kids some who hoped to get something again but the mood from the hunting scene wasn't right. I walked holding her hand and we started talking on other topics that were mood lifting. 'So everyone' I said. 'What makes you laugh? For me, hidden, witty comedy is good medicine especially if it is written, in that way I will form the image in my head to fit the occasion' 'I am more into visual comedy, I like acted scenes like of Mr Bean, stage comedy of Chris Rock, Steve Harvey and such also movies with Eddie Murpy, Martin Lawrence, Will Smith in movie scenes...' Don said 'I love those actors too' Tina said. 'I laugh at theater acts especially funny scenes acted from old books like for Shakespeare, also clowns and this short guy who never talks.....' she couldn't remember the name but she meant Charlie Chaplin 'also Robin Williams. We started giving the scenes that made everything funny. Black comedy took the bigger part since we were three blacks but we also knew the white comedians Nicole mentioned and we had a laugh, we had gone through the same broken part of the fence, down the slope into the botanical garden. It was around three o clock. There were many people in under the trees. 'I bet someone has had safari ants' bites.' Nicole said 'Nothing can make you undress so fast' we laughed remembering the morning scene. The garden was used for dates between students.

We had local comedians but they were not international yet, we could have shown them the videos which by the time were being quickly replaced by CDs locally. Internet was in very specific areas. In the university it was only in three places. One was the computer lab, then there were two cyber cafes, one was in faculty of arts and the other one was provided by African Virtual University (AVU) I don't think today such cyber cafes exist. Within ten years a lot changed with availability of cheap internet and affordability of computers and smart phones.

We could have sat down for some rest but we were better off gone to take each one a good shower. Don who lived within the campus staff housing branched off first. We said goodbye, we walked off as they talked hugging with Tina. Nicole held my hand more of leaning with it and looked up into my eyes. I am not sure she had looked at me for how many seconds but I sensed it and looked down at her. 'No one has done to me what you have' she said. 'You haven't taken me as an object not even once and I can't thank you enough for that. I think for once I can't tell my skin colour or yours, all I see is a great guy, I don't know what happens when I go back home, I come from a conservative white neighborhood and I only interacted with black people for the first time in college, it took long to know that they are just like us with different skin and maybe a different tradition, this happened in church groups. I can't assure you that we will meet again though I may come here as a tourist, it's a beautiful country and definitely with strange things happening inside the bushes but I like the diversity of it all.'

I had nothing to say, I knew with all my heart that if I could I would keep her or go with her but I was too young, what could I do at the age of nineteen, I had little to my name, college education ahead of me in a few months. This is something I could re visit after at least five years. 'It was great to meet you Nicole from Iowa, you have no idea what I feel when I imagine that in less than a week you will go back home' I said feeling it heavily in my heart. 'I know and sometimes in life things that we can't change happen. I wish I could give you more assurance but I can't' she wanted to say more but I said 'I am getting emotional and as an African man I prefer to smile than shed tears. You still have some more days let us celebrate them how we can' I said 'that works for me.' She said with tears in her eyes.

Tina caught up with us, we didn't talk much by the time they went through the gate to their hostel, I had to walk out of campus and I walked home in a melancholic mood. This was very confusing. Many guys believed that I will go to America soon, I knew there was no surety, what was obvious was that we were two young people in love but there was a race barrier, it was wide like the ocean that separated the our two continents.

My early memories and encounter with white people were very good memories. The first time I rode in a private car was with white couple. They had come to our church and they had mounted a projector screen in a different compound so I had gone with my brothers to watch. It was at night and I wondered how drivers knew the way at night. These white folks came with clothes to give us and sometimes we got very unique stuff, we associated white with good things. They carried honour and truthfulness, elegance and mannerisms. History from our parents and grandparents was still fresh of the dark days they endured during colonialism, how they lost land, put in detention and lost land. It was a new dawn where they came in a way to clean the name of the colonizers, these were Americans and the colonizer was Briton, same colour but very different mission. That time America was supposed to be like a village, I had no idea that it was across the ocean and a vast land.

As we came in as freshmen two months later, I skipped the orientation week, I knew every where within that campus, I would walk past the freshmen as if I was a senior. The senior years joined four or five days later officially but some especially men came early to have a look at the fresh girls, this was like the custom. These young men also wanted to have girl friends from this group; it was the first time they felt free to.

New students came in all colours and backgrounds. Some came in posh cars al though by this time rich student opted for private universities but they didn't have all courses; others came from very humble backgrounds; without student loans they couldn't manage. Some came from cities as I mentioned others you needed a larger map to locate their homes. From the cities there were categories too, some came from good quiet neighborhoods while others had ghetto written all over them, the two groups never mixed. There were also villagers who were city wannabes, they had relatives in urban areas and so they connected with the urban than the upcountry.

There were also country side folks that one doubted if they came from the countryside. They came from rich families so they had access of fine stuff. Most had gone to the best high schools and mingled and they afforded trendy clothes, this group mixed well in the campus. Last but not least there was guys like me, fate had brought us to an environment where we had learned to be in college before we were in college, we came in looking for business opportunities than seek the education. We had seen it all apart from being in lectures; we had cheered university teams even participated in jeering the opponents.

Some of us had been shaped by high schools to smoothen out the lingo that mattered. We had previously gone for university functions even dances, one of them was being registered by Emma, she was a young lady who was a promoter of a certain club while still student. When some were watching the student loan as a ritual some were making good money while still students. She was my fruits customer, a regular one and when she saw me she liked the fact that I was going. There was student centre restaurant the same one that was next to the gym. The guys that cooked and served food were all in, when we went to the function and a dedication was given in recognition of the campus they were the ones who shouted most. None of them had stepped into the high school but time had made them believe that they belonged which was sometimes good and sometimes deceiving. When Emma saw me around she said 'if you haven't paid, am paying for you but you are going with us'

It was good for I saw a guy who left the restaurant and looked presentable enough to work in a fancy restaurant as a waiter. He had taken in the experience well and behaved learned and confident enough to ask for such a job. Deceiving since these guys never graduated, I found them working in the restaurant and left them working there, no real progress in their lives, students came and students left and they were always there celebrating being part of the university fraternity.

From a general look I could tell with eighty percent accuracy who belonged to which category; I had seen them and interacted with them. I could tell who was there for learning only and any social life is a distraction to their goals, I could see young men who were already thirsty for a drink, those who wanted to have girls soonest possible salivating over them with hungry eyes, girls who belonged to Christian union and those who couldn't last another week without being hooked up especially when the other students arrived. I could tell leaders who already walked with some extra confidence. I could see the untouchable so to say, ladies who needed no ones love or attention unless you prove beyond reasonable doubt that you are worth your salt, more like Angie type and young men who seemed legal, they came wearing spectacles mostly, well dressed and in many cases they drove their parents to the campus. Within a week you could tell the sports guys, they would know where all sports took place, some came well built having been to the gym after high school, they walked as if they could pounce on ignorant niggas who were already smelling of cheap cigarettes and they did pounce on them when they collided.

Without being told, you could tell those who came from national or big high schools, they had many amenities so they came being good at some sports like rugby, basketball and swimming was only from the affluent schools. Now some remained the way they came in but some changed within a semester, some girls who came in looking very country changed and became like urbanites. Some young men also changed; some even poked their ears and completely changed their dressing style. Everything was to accomplish something, to some it worked well for others it blew up. Some had been caught stealing to sustain a life style for drinking or entertaining girls they couldn't afford.

Girls found themselves aborting or giving birth and living outside the campus which was very hard for some. Some girls became drunkards and I saw some who went close to clinical depression. Some played around and failed exams and they would realize that their drinking mates who would be boyfriends in the senior years passed.

Social classes were played even on Christian cycles, there were two groups that hardly mixed, this is for Pentecostal ones; urbanites didn't talk in tongues and had no overnight prayers. They were at par with new songs while the country folk were more spiritual you could even detect it in their dressing, they were conservative in all social activities; some crossed and hanged Christianity to have some fun, some suffered in the process, it was a territory they were not familiar with so some girls got pregnant and some men became too much to prove they are not Christianity. All I could say is God is not mocked, stick to your lane and under His grace, you came in as Christian remain like that.

Here freedom was fully exercised so unless very careful you would learn the hard way that the least lesson one learned was in lecture halls, there were social lessons everywhere, financial lessons too budget your money or you start begging for food before long. Love lessons were paramount; don't take someone like a spouse unless proven by time. Some lived as couples, it was prohibited but some hostels were hard to track those who did, they were former staff houses so manning their entrances was hard. Almost none of the campus couples married after college, even those who had a kid together. Some who met towards later in life are the ones who got married; few ones took the parenting responsibility like men. When we met as a class I was disinterested especially with girls, when we met for common a course I didn't ask who is who. Some guys asked for hostels and phone numbers, I could just walk without caring, my had was abroad somewhere, every now and then I would go to check my emails, by then phones were just calling toys.

Lecturers recognized me or related me with my brother, continuing students called me by name so I confused fresh men. How do these guys know me within weeks? One day after classes as I walked I noticed this girl walking beside me. I had seen her severally, she wanted to be noticed but I had not 'noticed' her, I was an enigma to her and she wanted to know me, 'hi, I am yet to know your name' she said. I knew her name; she had been discussed by my friends in my presence, she was called aloud many times while I was near as well. She knew me by name I was sure but she wanted a formal introduction. 'I don't know you either so we are even' I said with little interest. 'Every body in this class knows my name but I am Sharon just in case you haven't heard' she stretched her hand and shook mine; it was a little hand from a short, extra curved, good looking girl. Her eyes were not happy when for the first time I looked directly into her, she was faking the freshman celebrity status; this fame she was looking for was to hide something. 'Julian' I said still studying her eyes and instead of seeing the girl who desperately wanted to be noticed I felt compassion 'glad to meet you' her mouth smiled but her eyes did not, she told me where she came from and I told her that I was basically in my neighborhood. 'That's why even lecturers know you' she observed.

She never thought that was possible but I told her that all around the university were homes even where it looked commercial, people lived behind those commercial plots. Without asking she told me her hostel name and number and told me that I could visit. It was a Friday and she said that if I was available we could link up so we could talk more. For another guy this could have been music to his ears, there was no better invitation from a girl. I was busy that evening doing nothing in particular and I never visited her. She was lonely but not for a man in particular, she needed love and a connection that I doubted she could get from young men, she wanted to be famous within campus but she missed some charisma or simply she couldn't unmask in the process.

This was a case to many people who were emotionally needy, some wanted to run from a background that haunted them, others from prisons that were brought by labels they had from their families, some were healing from emotional scars, I wasn't off the hook on this, I wasn't a happy freshman, I was emotionally drained, I wanted to be with Nicole not with all these ladies combined, maybe it showed in my eyes maybe it did not. I avoided parties for two years apart from the class based ones, some wanted to lead and be recognized but they had no followers while some were hand picked to be class leaders, it was in them more than by chance; this is life with all its fairness and this goes beyond the physical looks.

Emotionally unstable people were not good for relationship, some were taken advantage of; my two roommates Kim and Andy at one time were dating roommates. Both girls were very emotional you could only learn that after being close to them. Marion was one and Yunis was the other, both very beautiful and had a classy look but Kim realized that his girl was an emotional wreck, she was so needy and he cut it off, she became so stressed so Andy invited her to join them as they went clubbing that weekend. Marion was also emotionally unstable but Andy wanted her like that, he wanted a needy lady to manipulate; now they were two vulnerable ladies to console. On the dance floor when Marion was seated Andy became too physical with Yunis and she responded, their lips made a long contact. Marion saw this and was broken as Yunis started to heal; it was such a crazy web that ended up in tears, both girls somehow dropped out of campus and Andy felt no loss.

There was another category that came to the campus like the young man from the indigenous tribes from the North, he came in ladies shoes and he was not trying to be funny. He was totally oblivious of the community he had joined, to say the least such an institution was a representation of the best brains in the country as far as education was concerned; this guy talked a lot and lied a lot if you were keen for a minute. Maybe he also had an inner baggage he tried to cover up. No body seemed to ask him about the shoes but I did. 'Why are you wearing ladies shoes?' he actually thought that I was asking somebody else but he realized some guys looked at his and smiled some not believing that I actually asked.

What's wrong with people? It was just a question that I needed an answer for but they looked away smiling. 'These are very expensive shoes, maybe you have not seen them yet, and they are for men but can also be unisex' he said as he looked at our disapproving faces. He wasn't fooling anyone. We knew expensive shoes and wore when we afforded them, that time timberland for a man was quite a statement in college. 'Are they?' I asked now with a smile 'show me another man with a shoe like that, with such a big sole and raised heel in this campus then I will believe you, how do you even walk?' I simply added. 'I imported this shoe from....' He was badly dressed with crumpled shirts and trousers that he seemed to sleep in; he was always with a crazy lie. 'You need help, you are delusional......' It was just at the beginning of a class and we settled down. He actually thought that he convinced all of us. Some ignorance doesn't belong to at institution of higher learning. Somehow someone always defied that by doing or saying something dumb. The guy at some point just disappeared from college and this happened to several guys who just stopped coming to college and quit. I don't know where they went, one time I met a classmate who dropped out, he couldn't remember me. I asked why he dropped out and he told me that he became a parent and opted out.

On the Eve of Nicole's departure she came to the stall and asked me if I would stay late we hang out. Some few other students had arrived and she was taking them around. They were just four from the same university but on graduate programs. I agreed; it was a pleasure to spend most of the night with her. The thought that she would go was hard enough, the fact that we both didn't know what happens after the day after was unthinkable but it was a fact that I was black and she was white. My day was very sad and I was melancholic about the whole situation, I was not about to hate my colour or where I was born. I couldn't regret meeting and falling in love with the girl either.

'I would love to stay late tonight, I wouldn't miss it for the world' I said. She was nervous that I could give an excuse for not being available, some people don't like goodbyes. I didn't mind it. She wasn't flying the following day but the whole group was to travel the country for three days then fly out. They were to visit maasai Mara game reserve for a game drive and a prehistoric site, then have one more day at the capital city near the airport. Don came to my stall and shared his discomfort too about Tina leaving. They duo had become good friends and close to both of us. We talked a lot on what we wished would happen in a perfect world. His case was different; there was no skin colour barrier, just the cultural one. Don was so much into going to the US but for me it wasn't about the place, it was about the person.

The evening came and Nicole was there to help me close up the stall, she looked at how I kept records, she was even observing how I write, we never got enough of stares every time she was with me. One senior student thought that she was doing a research that needed my stall when he passed by, he came pretending to buy something to really establish that we were friends. He came at the right time; Nicole was really goofing with me and looking at me with the eyes that don't need much explanation. He tried talking to her but he was the case of too much mother tongue interference. Ever listened to some Nigerians talking in English that sounded exactly like the mother tongue?. Nicole kept looking at me to know what he said and it was embarrassing that a senior student needed the fruits guy to pass his message. He was smoking and when the wind changed the smoke got to her, 'please can you stand far' she pleaded, she was coughing and I asked him to move away, 'I see you have won the lottery' he said in Swahili. 'I looked at him and asked 'how is that?' He smiled slyly wishing he was me and left.

Some guys thought it was exciting others thought it wasn't fair for them. Isn't that the normal with humans? Some will be happy for you others will be jealous. One girl found us at the stall and she was really happy that she took longer than necessary admiring the black and white couple. We happened to have green jackets, her favourite colour was green and I just happened to have a jungle green jacket at the time. She loved it because of the colour and I did love it coz it was warm, we looked matching which was by coincidence. She helped me pack and store all the fruits. I gave her some fruits some we ate some we carried to Don and Tina.

We walked hand in hand towards the nice restaurant by the pool although the pool was enclosed and no one could access it at night, we sat where the pool was well visible. Some guys had drowned in the pool at night; it was suicide due to campus stress. I knew one of them, a son of a professor who drowned in drugs and alcohol before he drowned his life. He was a lively slim tall boy, we were shocked that all this time he was making jokes he was suicidal; it looked beautiful at night, the restaurant was at a raised level and the view was clear. I wasn't hungry but it was a cold evening, I had to keep warm. We had dinner; most of it was done silently. We had chosen to sit on the sofa instead of dining type of chairs. She chose to sit beside me rather than across me. Once we were done we took take away coffee, we were to meet Tina and Don in the Lounge in the same building on a different floor but we chose to do the last walk as we sipped coffee. We needed time alone; we walked not very far like the last time but just a big tarmacked circle around departments and to the lounge. We found a bug the same type we had found before, I caught one for Nicole and she tied it using her hair. We walked in with it to the lounge and Tina ran to the far end begging Nicole to throw it out. It was hilarious for all of us, we didn't know much about phobias; I actually thought that some people just pretend to be afraid now I know better.

We sat in the lounge that had beige coloured quality fabric sofas, it was a nice dim lit room fully carpeted wall to wall; the lights were covered with antique lamp shades that brought out a mustard yellow illumination. This was not a student hang out but it was ok for the foreign students and since we accompanied them we were welcome. Mostly lecturers and other senior staff relaxed here. There was a bar in the next room and with seats just at the counter so the rest would come to the lounge. It was a decent type where by being rowdy would have you sent out and that's why they never allowed the students to hang out there. Student leaders did for their meetings and even relaxation; they had the diplomatic pass into it. As you come in from the main entrance there were glass slide windows straight on besides the hall way that led to the lounge. This part was raised and once the girlfriend to the student leader of the time missed steps after drinking one too many. She tried to get hold of the glass window for support but the windows were open, she took a tumble and fell on the flowers eight feet below.

She screamed loudly before she hit the ground, her friend noticed too late, she went for the legs but it was too late. Alarmed guys went round to the steps rushing to help her; the fear was if she had fallen head fast on the concrete foot path below, luckily she had tried to hold back so she dropped directly below, her head dug into the wet soil and her leg hit the concrete. She sprained her leg and got bruises on her face and back, her blouse got torn most of the back and she looked like a mess. It had rained early in the evening, the mud was on her face and the weave looked like she had been electrified; her make up was buried inside the mud. The student leader arrived; he had been clearing the bill when this happened. The lady was tall and heavy, she must have been over a hundred kilos. Men lifted her up; being drunk and hurt took several guys to get her up. She was taken directly to the university sanatorium. The student leader wasn't happy; this wasn't going well with his reputation, he was the guy who campaigned talking deep English and quoting Winston Churchill and other historical leaders until his classmates wondered where he learnt from. He had been very eloquent and smooth making his opponents inadequate by far, he walked with two guys as his body guards all the time; I don't know how they were paid or how much they were paid. They wore suits just like him; it sent the message home that as he walked around campus he was not just another bloke.

Those who saw her had their share of laughter separately and collectively when they remembered how a classy lady became a spectacle within seconds. Those who heard about it laughed again and it depended on who gave the story, some exaggerated until it became very funny. One guy said that the nurses had run away the moment she walked into the sanatorium thinking it was an animal prank.

The politics in the campus were dirty and tribal just like the national ones. They were rigged and votes were bought. Quacks got in on tribal plat forms leaving out some good people who were level headed. Student union leaders became drunk with power, money from the allowances and bribes to allocate student centre shops, free hostel rooms and girls. Some forgot that they were students that were at the mercies of the senate once they were found culpable. A good number never graduated or were suspended and came back with their tails between their legs. Freeloaders always lurked around them for loans that were never paid, to feed and drink. They walked an inch taller and ate for free at the student centre's restaurant or shops. They took shopping and other stuff like sodas and never paid.

One my classmate became a leader; I saw the transformation with my own eyes. We lived in the same hostel his room just nearby; best hostels in the campus; they all lived in there once elected. It was the best address for men that sometimes ladies never turned away an invitation. In this dude's kitchen were bottles of sodas that he never bought and never returned the bottles. With Dan another classmate we decided to take away all the bottles. Dan would put on a long coat and I would go to talk the leader praising him for his mission that never came to pass. Dan would enter the kitchen and steal many bottles that we sold in the shops at the student centre. It never felt like stealing since technically they were not his bottles and we weren't sure the specific shops where he took them from, we were benefitting for electing him and campaigning for him.

Power overcame him and he forgot to attend classes, along the way he rubbed shoulders with the Vice chancellor leading him to be dismissed. He was lucky he was able to go to the neighbouring country and attended a private university where he kept a low profile all the way to his PhD, many students thrown out were not as lucky, private university are expensive so you must have a sponsor.

The big girl limped for weeks and missed some classes, it was a warning that she should not just drink just because someone was buying. She also took longer to totally heal on the face scratches. It was embarrassing for the student leader, word spread like wild fire; he was even summoned at the senate to explain what happened. Senate took opportunities to sit and get allowances so grilling a student leader to embarrass him was joyful. Student leaders were always at logger heads with the administration. Such meetings had them expelled from campus; one minute you are at the top of the world the next you don't even have a place to sleep.

It was until around two in the morning that we decided to call it a night. We walked the girls down to their fancy hostel and Nicole asked me to wait at the balcony because she had some gifts for me, she brought me some carved animals, one was an elephant without the white the tusks. 'The missing white tusks will remind you of me while I am away' she said. She had written a note thanking me for being such a wonderful friend to her. Emotions overcame me and I shed tears, she did it too. We had to say good bye. Tina and her company were sitting in the curb by the flowers.

Earlier in our conversations, Nicole had asked me 'what makes you cry?' 'I don't cry; this is Africa men don't cry' I had said feeling manly. She had lived to see me cry. I just didn't know what could make me cry. My legs were very heavy walking away, I avoided looking back but I knew she was watching me since the door had not been closed. A few metres away I found Tina with Don and we hugged and said good byes.

I never slept and my day was a ship wreck. Tears just came to my eyes all day long. There were still two days before they left the country, they knew their itinerary and I made a decision to see her just one more time, I had to travel to the capital and go to the airport just to see her off but I wanted it to be secretly, just a glimpse of her to bring a closure to this.

The flight was around two, I was outside departure area where other friends and relatives saw off each other. It was an emotional area, some parents saw kids off to colleges and visitations, some kids saw off parents that would be gone for years to study or work. I was in sunglasses since my eyes were still teary. They came in a group; I noticed the university shuttle bus as it brought them to the parking. She was emotional as well; twice I saw her wipe off her eyes as she pulled her bag. She was not looking at the sides and I had planned to remain hidden. She went through the glass door and that's when she instinctively turned and looked directly at me just when I had removed the glasses, she was not allowed to come out once through the checking in door, she broke into sobs and she was comforted by her friends as they looked at me through the glass door. I waved at her blew a kiss and regretted coming to the airport. It would be a long ride back home.

Immediately she landed home she wrote me an email, we kept communicating everyday. She sent me her family photo later after all the photos we had taken, some post cards too. The communication went on almost through my time in college then it stopped and she just disappeared and she was not on social media and not answering any mail. I knew it was over, to me it was all about colour of our skins; it kept coming up in the mails how close family members were hard to like hear of a black guy being one of them or how condescending something was discussed while it involved a black celebrity but maybe there was another reason that I will never know she never said, it is a little world some people know where everyone should be of one skin colour; what you can I do apart from wish her well. We might meet in this lifetime if not, in the next.

www.ingramcontent.com/pod-product-compliance
Lightning Source LLC
LaVergne TN
LVHW050314160826
845677LV00014B/3387

* 9 7 9 8 7 6 6 1 2 1 2 5 1 *